OURAY

By P. David Smith

WESTERN REFLECTIONS, INC.

ISBN 1-890437-11-5

Western Reflections Publishing®
219 Main Street
Montrose, CO 81401
westref@montrose.net
www.westernreflectionspub.com

Third Edition

Cover and text design by Laurie Goralka Design

Table Of Contents

About the Author

P. David Smith, lawyer, Ouray County Judge and proprietor of Buckskin Trading Company (The San Juan History Store) has long had an interest in San Juan history. He has written five other book on Colorado history — *Mountain Mysteries: They Ouray Odyssey, The Million Dollar Highway, Ouray: Chief of the Utes, Mountains of Silve: The Story of the Red Mountain Mining District* and *Images of the San Juans.* He is a past president of the Ouray County Historical Society and lectures frequently on Colorado history.

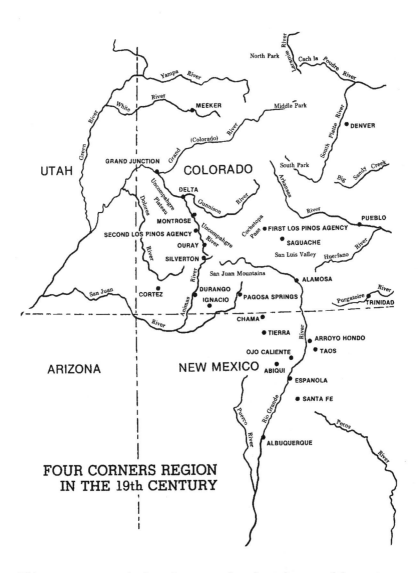

This map represents the Four Corners region about the turn of the century. The entire area covered by the map represents the territory controlled by the Ute Indians before the arrival of the white man.

CHAPTER ONE

Before There Was A Town

For centuries prior to the arrival of the white man, the Tabeguache Utes traveled into the region now known as Ouray. It is inaccurate to say that they "lived" there because the Utes were highly nomadic and moved their camps constantly in the summer. In the winter the local Utes stayed in the lower elevations. One favorite spot was in the vicinity of the junction of the Gunnison and Uncompahgre rivers near the present-day town of Delta. However in the summer, spring and fall the beauty of the imposing bowl or amphitheater that later came to hold the City of Ouray certainly appealed to the Utes as much as it does today to the hundreds of thousands of tourists who visit the city every summer.

Three large waterfalls (including Ouray's famous Box Canyon Falls) are either inside the present-day Ouray city limits or are located only a short distance away. Five creeks flow into the Uncompaghre River within the boundaries of the town. Because of the tremendous geologic activity in the San Juans, the steep and multi-colored cliffs around Ouray expose millions of years of geologic history. The amphitheater itself was carved out of a large dome of volcanic tuff by glaciers — a few of which hung around until as recently as 10,000 years ago. Although the great bowl is composed of volcanic material, it is not the remains of an ancient volcano; rather it was ice, not fire, that caused its present shape.

Abundant deer, elk and Rocky Mountain sheep have always scrambled around the local mountainsides. Several hot springs surface within the city limits, undoubtedly used and enjoyed as much by the Ute Indians as by current visitors. An especially sacred place for the Utes was the hot springs located about one mile south of Ridgway. The springs meant so much to the Utes that when they ceded the San Juans in 1873, they put a special provision in the treaty that if the springs were found to be on American land (south of the 38th parallel), they would nevertheless continue to belong to the Utes. The Utes knew the curative, relaxing powers of the hot waters and enjoyed a relaxing time in God's wonderland as much as we do. As soon as the government surveyors arrived, they discovered that the springs were, in fact, south of the 38th parallel. Therefore what became known as "the four-mile strip" was given back to the Utes. This consisted basically of the northern two-thirds of the valley between Ouray and present-day Ridgway.

The Tabeguache were one of seven bands of Utes which together roamed over what is now known as Colorado, eastern Utah and northern New Mexico. Each band had its own favorite territory, but they didn't hesitate to venture into land controlled by the other Ute bands. They were brave and ferocious fighters who repeatedly defended their homeland from attacks by neighboring Indian tribes. However the Utes were also one of the first tribes to establish relations with the Spanish and later the Americans. In great part this was due to a desire to assimilate items into Ute culture that could make their life easier. First and foremost was the horse, but firearms and iron tools were also of great importance. By the time the whites actually arrived in what came to be Colorado Territory, the Utes were leading an easy enough life. It could be said that they seemed to be enjoying an idyllic time in an awe-inspiring land.

The Utes' lifestyle was dramatically improved when they obtained the horse from the Spanish settlers in New Mexico. Of almost equal importance was the acquisition of firearms.

The local Utes were eager to serve as guides for the Juan Maria de Rivera expedition in 1765 and for Friars Escalante and Dominguez in 1776. Both expeditions passed through present-day Ouray County while trying to find a route from Sante Fe to California. The Utes were quick to show the explorers their trails and the easiest ways to ford the rivers or cross the mountainous barriers; however, the desired route was never found. When the official Spanish expeditions of Rivera and Escalante came to Colorado they found most of the prominent geographic features had already been given Spanish as well as Ute names (for example the Uncompahgre River was called "Rio de San Francisco"), all of which indicated that illegal Spanish gold seekers had been in the area for some time.

One famous trail became the main route out of the San Luis Valley into

Utah. It was used from ancient times and ran, in part, on top of the Ouray Amphitheater. Remnants of 6,000 year old Clovis points and Spanish armor have been found along the route which became known as Horse Thief Trail because of the major source of its traffic. Later on when fur trappers came to the Uncompahgre Valley, the Utes were more than willing to share their game and to allow intermarriage with their women. However, when hoards of whites poured into their territory after the discovery of gold in 1859, the Utes realized that their occupation of the land was in danger, and they began to resist what they saw as an invasion by the whites.

Chief Ouray (front middle) and four of his important subchiefs posed for this photograph during the treaty negotiations of 1880, but all of those in the picture were also involved in the 1868 and 1873 treaties.

It was in large part through the efforts of the Ute Chief Ouray that all out war was avoided. Ouray realized that the whites enormously outnumbered the Utes, and he tried to keep their land through treaties and negotiation instead of by force. Although he eventually failed, he won the love and respect of the whites at the same time that he held onto the Utes' land for much longer than anyone expected. In 1873 the Utes agreed to allow the whites to take posses- sion of the San Juan Mountains, while retaining most of their land to the west and north. For the next five years whites lived in the southern half of present- day Ouray County, while Ute land began just a few miles north of the City of Ouray. The City of Ouray was established and named in Ouray's honor just a few years before his death. In 1881 the Utes were removed from Colorado except for a small reservation along the southwest boundary of the State.

When tens of thousands of prospectors swarmed into Colorado (then part of Kansas Territory) in 1859 and 1860, they soon discovered that there was not nearly enough potentially rich mineral land in the vicinity of the initial discoveries at Clear Creek on the eastern slopes of the Rocky Mountains. They soon spread out over most of Colorado Territory, and by 1861 white men were camping in what became Ouray County. The prospectors came to Ouray over yet another old Ute trail which ran across Cochetopa Pass and passed near the present-day cities of Gunnison and Montrose. They made small strikes of placer gold near the current Ridgway Lake, and several parties of men were eventually panning for gold in the Uncompahgre River. However the prospectors also discovered the winter temperatures to be milder in the amphitheater of present-day Ouray and a small party of men spent the winter there in 1861-62. We now think of the 1880s or 90s as "roughing it." The May 30, 1890 *Solid Muldoon* included an interview with O. H. Harker who first came to the Ouray bowl in May of 1861 with the Wright party which came from Ft. Garland via Cochetopa Pass. Mr. Harker is quoted as saying, "It took nerve and staying qualities to prospect the San Juan in those days."

MINING IN COLORADO.

This early day engraving represents the kind of terrain that early prospectors were supposedly dealing with in Colorado; however, it slightly exaggerates the ruggedness of the mountains.

Several fascinating stories of lost gold arose out of such incidents, including a legend that two disillusioned California prospectors spent the winter in the Ouray valley somewhere around 1863. The men were cautious of the Utes and realized that they could be risking their lives if they were captured. Eventually they found traces of gold in Oak Creek and supposedly traced it to a ledge "of almost pure gold." Winter was coming on fast and they were low on food, so the prospectors decided to build a large fire against the ledge and then throw cold water on the heated rock to crack it and allow removal of the gold. The technique worked, but it also attracted the attention of the Utes. The men fled with the small amount of gold that they were able to carry. They told many others of their find, but no one yet has discovered the fabulous golden ledge.

This newspaper print was labeled "Dangers of Prospecting — A Scene in the Rocky Mountains." It could well have occurred in the vicinity of Ouray. (Frank Leslie's Illustrated Newspaper, February 13, 1886).

In the summer of 1875 the Tabeguache Ute Indian Agency was transferred from the original site near Cochetopa Pass to a place on the Uncompaghre River near present-day Colona. Besides Henry F. Bond, the Indian agent, several other white men accompanied the Utes to act as cowpunchers, blacksmiths, and teachers. They explored far up the Uncompahgre River to present-day Ouray and reported that several "discovery" cuts had been made in the hills by prospectors. They also noticed that rough bridges had been constructed in many places where the Ute trails crossed creeks or ravines. A sawmill was set up at the new Ute agency and a good many Mexican laborers were brought in to make 300,000 adobe bricks for the agency buildings. Logging camps were also established in the vicinity to bring in timber for the new sawmill.

By the end of the summer the agency's cow camp had also been moved across the Cochetopa Trail to what became known as Cow Creek. Beef was now on hand to supply the Utes, the agency workers and sometimes local prospectors. It is said that Chief Ouray himself chose the spot for the cow camp because of its long, lush grass. The cowboys noted numerous signs that white men had long been in the area, including well-used and abandoned wagon hubs, picks and shovels. The cowboys built a corral and cabin near the junction of Cow Creek and the Uncompahgre (near the present Ridgway Dam). One day they discovered the 1875 Wheeler governmental survey crew temporarily camped nearby as they finished up their work.

The Los Pinos II agency was located near present day Colona. Building A was the agent's house. Buildings B and D are for storage, while C was a dwelling and mess hall for the employees. (Harper's Weekly, October 25, 1879).

In the early 1870s the United States government had decided that surveys should be made of the vast lands in the West that were being incorporated into the country as territories or states. The Wheeler Survey was authorized to prepare detailed maps of the San Juans by the United States War Department in 1873. The survey party made its way into the San Juans from the south and west in 1874 and again in 1875. The Hayden survey expedition was also sent to explore the San Juans by the Department of the Interior during that time, they set out from Silverton in

1875 and went up Mineral and Cement creeks into what we now call Ironton Park. In August William Marshall of the Wheeler Survey noted a new mining town to be already in existence in Red Mountain (Ironton) Park, which he believed to be called "Park City." Although very short lived Park City was probably the first settlement in Ouray County. Marshall concluded that the route down the Uncompahgre Canyon towards present-

The ownership of this house has caused great debate in Ouray. Some say that it is Chief Ouray's house, built before the whites even came to the Ouray bowl. Others feel that it is simply an early settler's cabin.

In the early 1870s the United States government sent surveyors all over the western part of the nation to chart what had been wilderness. These two men were members of the Hayden Survey Party.

day Ouray was "utterly impassable," although he did climb Mount Hayden and look down into the amphitheater valley.

These prospectors are looking for signs that they may have struck it rich. They evidently haven't decided yet, but the man on the left looks as if he may have given up hope. (Harper's Weekly, November 10, 1883).

In July of 1875 A . W. Begole and John Eckles entered the heavily wooded Ouray amphitheater from the south, having come down Bear Creek from Engineer Mountain. It was a much more difficult route than from the north, but it had the advantage of not passing through Ute territory and being much closer to "civilization" at nearby Silverton. On the way back to Silverton via the Poughkeepsie Gulch-Red Mountain route, they met other men whom they told of their discovery. Soon there were several dozen men headed for the Ouray amphitheater. Begole and Eckles returned with other prospectors about a month later. A. J. Staley and Logan Whitlock, who had actually been on a hunting and fishing expedition, discovered the Trout and Fisherman lodes on August 23, 1875. They were the first mining claims of any great worth in what became the Uncompahgre Mining District, and the first shipments of ore from the Ouray area came from their mine. Perhaps it was appropriate that fishermen also discovered the first real mine in Ouray, as recreation and mining have always been the city's largest industries. Begole, Jacob Ohlwiler and John Morrow had earlier located the Cedar and Clipper mining claims within the present-day city limits on August 11, 1875, but they never proved to be of any great mineral value. In October of 1875 Begole and Eckles discovered the Mineral Farm mine about a mile southwest of the new settlement. The mine took its name from the parallel veins that ran on the surface so as to be worked much as a farmer might dig potatoes at his farm. It was an extremely rich discovery and so close to town!

It was obvious that the strikingly beautiful Ouray bowl would make a perfect town site in the rugged San Juans. Not only was its surface relatively flat, but it was also the only outlet into the Uncompahgre Valley. The many hot springs made the site considerably warmer than the surrounding territory. On August 28, 1875 the town site of "Uncompahgre City" was laid out by Begole, Eckles, M. W. Cline, R. F. Long, A. J. Staley and Logan Whitlock and surveyed by D. W. Brunton, who was an engineer who happened to be in the area. Cline and Long took up residence on the town site almost immediately, even driving stakes into the densely wooded forest to indicate alleys and streets, but Uncompahgre City never became more than a paper town. The name had been picked for the Ute word for the area which means "warm or hot springs."

While the men from Silverton were prospecting around the Ouray amphitheater, other prospectors, who would eventually play just as large a role in the history of Ouray, had come over Red Mountain Pass, then up and over Imogene Pass and into Imogene Basin. Andy Richardson, who was prospecting with David P. Quinn, named the pass and the basin after his wife and staked claims in most of the basin. At this time his discoveries were only low grade gold and silver, but at a later date the richest strikes in the vicinity of Ouray would be made in Imogene Basin. W. H. Brookover and brothers George and Edward Wright headed into Yankee Boy Basin. Brookover and Edward Wright discovered the Wheel of Fortune Mine in October of 1875. It was an extremely rich discovery which showed an eighteen to twenty inch vein of up to 1200 ounces of silver and twenty ounces of gold per ton in early assays. The first large load of ore sent out from the mine ran 640 ounces of silver per ton. Most of these men spent the winter of 1875-76 in these bowls, completely unaware that other men were at a lower elevation close by. Richardson's cabin even came to be shown as a small settlement on local maps.

Several men stayed in the Ouray bowl during the winter of 1875-76. There were also women with the group and in November of 1875 a Captain Butler's wife gave birth to what was claimed to be the first white child born in the city. (In these days the women themselves were never named as giving birth — it was always so-and-so's wife who made the delivery as if the women themselves had little to do with it.) Judge Long, Captain Cline and the Cutler brothers agreed to go to back to civilization to obtain supplies for those who were staying the winter. They arrived in Saguache on November 7, 1875, and they left the same day with two wagons full of supplies. However they were stopped by the Utes near the

The Town of Silverton was Ouray's only real competition during the 1880s. It was bigger during that period, but seemed to be basically deserted when W. H. Jackson took its picture on this day.

The early day prospector's camp was primitive — his shelter, a tent; his chair, a rock; his oven, a pair of sticks and his table, a log. His only companions were often his burro and his dog. (Harper's Weekly, Nov. 10,1883)

top of Cochetopa Pass and told that they could not go across the reservation. They disobeyed the order and arrived in Ouray with supplies on December 7, 1875. Captain Cline then took the wagons back to Saguache loaded with ore from the Trout and Fisherman Mine.

These prospectors have just about everything needed to start developing a new mine — blasting powder, picks, shovels, a saw, a sledge hammer (called a double jack) and a variety of different sized drills.

Ouray's first post office was established October 28, 1875, but it was little more than a promise to have mail brought up from the Ute agency. Even though in 1875 the settlement was called "Uncompahgre", there is no record that the post office ever had any name other than "Ouray." The name "Uncompahgre" was used, however, for mail coming into the Los Pinos II agency. Otto Mears was awarded the contract to carry the mail to the Ute agency and it was distributed from that point to the various mining camps nearby. When the snow deepened Otto Mears tried dog teams to carry the mail. Eventually, to avoid losing the mail contract, he himself used snowshoes to bring the mail through. However it was a futile effort and Ouray's new post office closed March 20, 1876. It did reopen without further interruption on May 9, 1876.

Meanwhile at the Ute agency at the northern end of the county, Agent Rev. Henry F. Bond's household was reported to consist of "highly cultured people, whole-souled and cordial." There were fourteen employees at the new agency and they formed a literary, debating and dramatic club. For

Christmas of 1875 the employees shot a wild turkey. The inhabitants of Uncompahgre City celebrated Christmas in a less dignified manner. Judge Long and the Cutler brothers invited the locals up to their cabin located on a slight rise above the new settlement. Since no liquor was available, the men reportedly drank spoiled vinegar to get drunk and then christened the place "Vinegar Hill." The name has stuck to this day as Ouray's sledding hill.

Scenes like this were often seen in Denver and other large Colorado towns in the 1860s. The man in the back is probably telling the crowd about the riches of an area from which he has just returned.

Although Spring came early, there were not enough supplies stockpiled, and the Ouray prospectors nearly starved to death before new supplies arrived in early summer. The Ute agency had also completely run out of basic supplies like sugar, salt, candles and coal oil. Many of the prospectors fended off starvation that winter by illegally killing and eating the Utes' cattle. All unbranded cattle were termed "slow elk" by the prospectors and were considered fair game. So many cows disappeared that a financial cover up took place at the agency and eventually the Rev. Bond was requested to resign as agent. Major W. D. Wheeler (brother of the government surveyor) was appointed to replace him.

Both the whites at the agency and the Utes themselves became an important source of support for the new arrivals in Ouray. Those at the agency often came to town to trade or look around. The Utes would trade food and blankets to the settlers and horse races often were arranged between the two groups. However, Agent Wheeler also took the Utes' possession of the "four-mile strip" seriously. He constantly ran settlers off the land and even erected monuments declaring it to be Ute territory. The white settlers kept coming back. This was good farm land, only a few miles from Ouray. Many of the prospectors were causing problems for the Utes. Placer gold had been discovered near Ridgway. Several prospectors refused to leave, even when ordered to do so daily by the Utes or the agent. It was only after the whites determined that the area was worked out that they left on their own. It created quite some tension, and Agent Wheeler asked for troops to be sent to protect him. A small garrison under the command of Lt. John Conline was established at a location a few miles north of the Los Pinos II agency in 1877. A housewife, Mrs. W. B. Phillips, noted that the Utes were causing problems too. She lived on the American side of the reservation line and saw the Utes often.

> *We got along fine with them, except for one thing — we had to feed them whenever they wanted and they sure could eat. There were four or five hundred of them and they almost ate us out of house and home while we were there. One day a half dozen of them came into our cabin and ordered supper. We got it for them without much argument and after they had eaten they informed us that they had decided to stay all night. . . . In return for our enforced hospitality whenever we lost any cattle, they would find them for us.*

This engraving, entitled "Prospecting on the Ute Reservation — An Ominous Meeting" shows the tension that obviously still existed in 1879 between the whites and the Utes. (Harper's Weekly, Oct. 25, 1879)

For some unknown reason it was decided during the winter of 1875-76 that the name of the new town should be "Ouray" instead of "Uncompahgre." Perhaps it was a move to seek Ouray's protection or perhaps in thanks for the help he gave the settlers during that first rough winter. Visitors still question the correct way to pronounce the Chief's name. Since the Utes have considerable trouble making an "r" sound, it is quite likely that his name was originally pronounced Oo-lay or U-lay. His name was originally written in such a way. However the whites corrupted his name into You- Ray (in Spanish — "Ure") and Ouray accepted the change.

Chief Ouray and his wife, Chipeta, made a proud and striking couple. This photo was taken in Washington in 1880, just shortly before Chief Ouray's death. The "bows" on his shoulders are actually medicine pouches.

CHAPTER TWO

A Town Is Built

Those hardy individuals who spent the winter of 1875-76 in Ouray's grand bowl suffered many hardships, but there was one main goal that kept them going — they would be the first persons on the scene come spring. They knew there was almost as much money to be made by land speculation in a new town as there was from the rich minerals in the mountains. In the spring, as soon as the snow melted enough, Captain Cline returned from Saguache, and he brought thirty other men with him. Many others followed, and the rush was on. Ouray grew with absolutely amazing speed, as it was unceasingly promoted during the next few years. Local men who were traveling back East never lost the chance to talk of its beauty, its mines, its endless supply of timber and abundant game.

Making ready to leave the Winter camp.

These men are loading their burros with everything they could carry in the way of supplies, as they leave their winter camp to go prospecting high in the mountains. (Harper's Weekly, November 10, 1883)

In early spring of 1876 a Mr. Randall brought in a stock of groceries and started Ouray's first store out of Staley and Whitlock's log cabin. Staley and Whitlock themselves were already back in the hills looking for a new strike. Judge Stevens established a blacksmith shop in late May, 1876. This gave the prospectors a way to buy tools and sharpen their drill steel, as well as a means of shoeing the horses. He was joined in 1877 by Louis King, who was not only a blacksmith, but also an accomplished carriage maker. In June of 1876 Mr. and Mrs. Dixon started a hotel in their log cabin. She furnished the meals, but guests had to bring their own bedding, and they slept on the floor. Nate Hart opened the first saloon — which was always an important part of any new mining town. Jesse Benton, who later became a famous sheriff in Ouray, opened the first meat market. Benton also built the first frame building in Ouray that summer. On August 1, 1876 a man named Tanner opened a store in a tent, but he died soon thereafter and became Ouray's first burial. It is reported that the first death from disease or sickness in Ouray occurred in August of 1877, so it is presumed that Tanner died from an accident or died a natural death. Captain Cline was the first postmaster and he distributed the mail out of his small log cabin until a frame building was built for him in 1877. Now the courthouse stands on that spot. There was only a short centennial celebration in Ouray on July 4, 1876 and again when Colorado became the 38th state on August 1, 1876. There was simply too much work to do to spend time celebrating!

Louis King, who arrived in Ouray shortly after its founding, was a really good blacksmith and wagon maker. The miniature Overland Stage which he made for Ouray's children is a good example of his work.

On October 2, 1876 the town was officially incorporated, although the official survey by H. W. Reed wasn't completed until October 30, 1876. On September 13, 1876 the San Juan county commissioners (the town of Ouray was located in San Juan county at this time) approved a request by the citizens of Uncompahgre City that the new plat be accepted but now with the name "Ouray." Ira Munn, Robert Long, Theron Stevens, M. W. Cline and James Call were appointed the first board of trustees. They held their first meeting October 4, 1876 and appointed William Munn the town clerk. On January 25, 1877 M. W. Cline paid $375 to the United States government in exchange for title to Ouray's 300 acres. Speculation in the development of towns was indeed profitable as each of the first lots in town sold for that much or more!

Even about 1880, when this photograph was taken, the Town of Ouray was still full of stumps. There were no brick buildings yet, and the town had an unsteady and uncertain look about it.

However a problem soon occurred with the town's development. At the first town election held on April 2, 1877, the old town board was replaced by a new group of men. The defeated candidates wouldn't give up their seats and they wouldn't release the town's records. Both boards began issuing deeds to town lots; therefore, neither of the board's deeds was considered legal. A lawsuit resulted, but after many months of waiting the judge refused to act on the matter. Finally a citizens' group was formed, which forced an end to the controversy by making the first board give up control to the second board.

Ouray County was established from the northern part of San Juan County on January 18, 1877. Its boundaries were much bigger than present as it included all of present-day Ouray, Dolores and San Miguel counties. The first commissioners were H. J. Hammon, chairman, W. J. Buchanon and James Call. A. E. Long was elected County Clerk at the first meeting held March 7, 1877. The Town of Ouray was designated the county seat. The first county elections were held September 8, 1877. Among other actions the commissioners entered into an agreement with Jesse Benton to rent the second floor of his new frame building. The first floor was being used as a combination saloon, church and courtroom. The town of Ouray didn't have an official meeting place since it didn't build its first Town Hall until the early 1880s. At that time the city fathers' built a frame building across from the Beaumont and next to the Capitol Saloon. One of the town's hose carts stood out front and the log jail was in back. There were also hose carts scattered around Ouray at strategic locations.

Once again all of the residents of Ouray got together for a big celebration on Christmas Day, 1876. The women of the town served a wonderful dinner at "Fat" Chitty's butcher shop. A big dance was also held. So grand was the celebration, that several Silverton residents came over the pass to join the affair. Unfortunately they got caught in a snow storm on the way back and almost froze to death before arriving home three days later.

The winter of 1876-77 was also severe, and residents existed primarily on bread and coffee. Game was scarce and sometimes meat was not available for weeks at a time. Musty bacon rinds, sugar and dried apples were considered a luxury. From then on, the Ouray merchants learned to bring in huge stores of supplies for the winter. The big mines would usually buy their supplies in Denver, but the small mines and the town folks depended on the local merchants, who also grubstaked local prospectors, and usually made money on the propositions. In the spring, the stores were always crowded with prospectors who were buying their supplies for the summer.

In January of 1877 papers had to be filed with the United States Land Office to show that the town of Ouray was actually occupied. The report stated that the town had over 400 inhabitants, 214 cabins and tents, a school, two blacksmiths, two hotels, a sawmill, an ore sampling works, a post office, and four general merchandise stores. It avoided the less desirable data — that Ouray had seven saloons and more gambling places and houses of prostitution than the civilized inhabitants cared to count. On the weekends when the miners and prospectors came into town, its population might swell to over 1,000. However Ouray was far from being an actual town. The merchants, saloonkeepers, lawyers, grocers, hotel owners and even prostitutes knew that there was plenty of money to be made from the miners and prospectors that came down from the mining districts in the vicinity of the town, but they also knew that it was just as likely that the town would dry up and blow away in no time.

The freighter in this photo is bringing groceries to the high mountain mines, including several pig carcasses. The snow has evidently melted just enough to make springtime travel possible.

Transportation was not easy in those days. To the west the trails were passable only on foot or on horseback, and they were dangerous at that. A toll road to the north was incorporated by A. W. Begole, E. C. Bradley and J. T. Jones on November 3, 1876, but Otto Mears bought them out and actually constructed the road in 1877. He may well have taken the action because of his mail contract to Ouray and the difficulties that he had with getting the mail through in the past year. The Ouray toll road branched from Mears' Saguache to Lake City Toll Road and was very rough. Although the trip to Saguache by wagon was reduced from four weeks to two weeks, its patrons were constantly complaining that it shouldn't even be called a road, little less a toll charged! Mears' toll gate at the Ouray end was at Skyrocket Creek and a fence ran out on either side. The toll was high — twenty dollars for a six mule team wagon. Only heavy duty wagons or buckboards could use the road. Mears used his toll roads to his advantage in shipping goods to Ouray and soon opened both a hardware and grocery store.

There was also an early day toll road that started toward Mineral Point, but this one was not controlled by Mears, at least not yet. By the summer of 1877 a wagon road had been almost completed to Bear Creek Falls but it was very rough. The trail that continued on from there was reported to be unsafe even to those those walking, if it was wet weather. Several men actually fell to their deaths off the cliffs along the trail. It would take several more years, but Otto Mears also took control of and finished this road, which eventually came to be known as a part of the Million Dollar Highway.

The trails to the San Juan mines are correctly depicted by the ruggedness shown in this photo. Early prospectors had great difficulty getting into Ouray from the south. This site is a few miles south of Ouray and it's no exaggeration!

Ira Munn built the first sawmill in Ouray in 1877 in an area of town still known as Munn Park alongside the Uncompahgre River. Before that time what little sawn lumber that was available came from the Hotchkiss family sawmill near the Indian reservation. Ira and his brother, William Munn, also built a sampling works on the spot. It was one of several in town, which purpose was to take samples of the ore being shipped and come up with an averaged assay value so that the mine owners would know if they were being cheated by the mills or smelters.

Another sign of permanence was a newspaper. Volume 1, Issue 1 of the *Ouray Times* appeared on June 16, 1877. It was a Republican paper published by "H. Ripley and brother." The front page of the very first paper carried an article claiming that the government was soft on the Utes, as settlers in the "four mile strip" had been given only a six month extension to get out of Uncompahgre Park. As it turned out the settlers didn't move and continued to trespass on the Utes' land for many years. After toiling for over a month to get his heavy press, type and supplies from Canon City to Ouray (a distance of 300 miles) in a convoy of six wagons, Ripley announced:

> *Here we are. Have come with the expectation of making this home. In choosing this point as our location we were influenced by the same motives that influenced others, chief among which is that of the almighty dollar . . . . The town is yet sound and it will require the cooperation of all to make our enterprise a success, and the success of our enterprise means the growth and prosperity of the town.*

In August of 1878 Dr. L. C. McKinney and J. F. Dowling started a competing paper, The *San Juan Sentinel*, but because the Ripleys were well liked, the competing paper only lasted a few months.

Otto Mears and Chief Ouray posed for this photo in 1868. Mears was well respected by the Utes, in large part because he took the time to learn their complicated language.

Last, but not least, was the arrival of the preachers, who brought a sense of culture and dignity to the community. In mid-June three of them appeared on the scene at nearly the same time. They took turns preaching at the local saloons and the county courtroom, using beer and nail kegs for seats and the altar. They operated under the theory that "only the sick need a doctor." The paper was certainly proud of the ministers arrival.

The rapidity with which school houses and church organizations have recently been established here corroborates the statement I have just made of the character of society of Ouray and the evidence of good moral tone of its citizens and their appreciation of the divine and intellectual attainments.

Henry Ripley, Ouray's first newspaper editor, is at the center of this photograph. The Ouray Times building is the second from the left. The building at the right, in the far rear, is the infamous 220 saloon.

The Rev. George M. Darley had reached Ouray first on March 14, 1877, but he soon left. By summer he was back and organized a building fund for the Presbyterian church, which was officially started June 24, 1877. The church structure was actually dedicated October 14, 1877 as the first church building in Ouray. The Rev. A. B. Whitney held the first Baptist services on June 16, 1877. The Methodist minister, the Rev. C. L. Libby, was the first to announce that he would begin regular Sunday services, but all of the preachers dropped in and out of town at the time. Libby reportedly arrived in town half-frozen and holding on to the tail of his donkey because he was going snow blind. However half the preachers in Colorado reportedly arrived in various towns in such a manner.

St. John's Episcopal Church is on the left, the Delmonico Hotel at the center rear and the Methodist Church on the right. Ouray has supported many churches over the years.

Libby was quickly followed by Parson Hogg (pronounced Hoag) who established the Episcopal Church on July 29, 1878. The Episcopalians' building was finished February 7, 1880. It is presently the oldest church building in Ouray, since the Presbyterian church building was sold to the Catholics soon after its establishment and eventually moved to Nucla. The present Episcopal building is actually only the basement of the original plans, later converted to use as the church proper.

Miss Libbie King began Ouray's first school in a cabin at the top of Vinegar Hill in Ouray on June 18, 1877. The town was already crowded with children, and the school was badly needed. Its first term ran for three months and closed September 16, 1877. The first school superintendent noted that there were forty-three "puples" who at one time or another attended the "schol." Miss King continued to run the school for three month sessions with fifty to sixty students attending at least one day of each session.

Ouray's first structures were very temporary. Many were simply tents. The first men who arrived in Ouray were not particularly interested in looks, but were merely trying to provide protection from the elements as quickly as possible. The thick forests in the little bowl were quickly denuded as the settlers built log cabins. One favorite form of construction was to build four or five rows of logs and then finish the roof with planks which in turn could be covered tightly with a tarp. It made the roof very tight and waterproof. The structure also had the advantage of being quick to build and being highly portable except for the first rows of logs. However some log structures had disadvantages. A June of 1877 *Times* article reported, "Our jail leaks." Prisoners were knocking out the logs and escaping. The editor called for a new stone jail to be built immediately. It didn't happen.

A sawmill's crew took a break for the photographer; the man on the left probably being the proud owner. The sawmill allowed a new town to put flesh on its bones, since it was usually too expensive to ship in lumber.

The arrival of a sawmill within the town in 1877 was a sure sign that the town was gaining some permanence. There were even some bricks for sale at the time, but it was many more years before anyone spent the time or the money to build a brick building. Ouray's houses were still crude structures that had been hastily constructed with little or no foundation. Even though many were built directly on the ground, they still remain today because of the dryness of the climate. Ouray had the look of most early day boom towns — false fronted buildings and crooked log cabins. Many of the log cabins later had siding applied directly over the logs so as to give the dignified and fashionable appearance of a frame house.

With all the building going on, the town was soon full of stumps and only a few of the original fir or spruce trees remained. The town council had the street supervisor busy blasting stumps from the streets. Unfortunately, he entered into his task just a little too enthusiastically and nearly blew down several nearby houses. Small brass kerosene lamps were hung at major intersections to help light the streets at night. Men in each part of the town had their assigned lamp that they either lit or filled. In 1877, George Kimball, Charles Wheeler and James Vance put in the city's first water system. A log dam on Oak Creek diverted water into a ditch and carried it to a reservoir (no longer used) above Oak Street. Three of the town's largest hot springs were also arranged to make small pools for bathing. There was no cost, but the paper predicted that private citizens would soon take them over because of the medicinal qualities of the water.

By the beginning of 1878 Ouray's population had risen to close to eight hundred. Regular mail service had been established, but until July it arrived only once a week (in on Tuesdays, out on Wednesdays). The Times complained that Ouray "is on one end of the longest saddle bag mail route in the United States." The whites were also finally able to take the "Four-mile Strip" away from the Utes in 1878. The government really gave the Utes no choice, paying them $10,000 and taking the land even though they didn't want to sell. The Ute reservation then started near the present-day town of Ridgway. Perhaps as a sign from the angry Ute gods, an earthquake hit the land that was taken that year. It did little damage to the town, but the hot springs in Ouray and Ridgway both rose over ten feet in height.

The artist who drew this engraving in 1877 made many of Ouray's buildings larger than actual size, yet the town still looks half empty. The Dixon House is the large building at the center of the photo.

A different sign of permanence occurred when the Bank of Ouray, was incorporated June 14, 1877 by Milton Cline, Jack Ohwiler, H. F. Blythe and H. W. Broloski. It originally occupied a building between Third and Fourth streets on Sixth Avenue across from City Hall. The bank remained in existence until a few years after the Silver Crash of 1893. Ouray's second bank was formed June 8, 1878 and named the Miners and Merchants' Bank by the founding Thatcher Brothers of Pueblo, who owned a chain of banks in the major mining districts throughout Colorado. E. J. Bent managed the bank for the Thatchers. When it was completed, the Miners and Merchants later moved to the southwest corner of the Beaumont Hotel and remained there for many years.

The town celebrated the 4th of July, 1877 in a big way. A huge 13 by 20 foot flag was made by Mrs. M. W. Cline and Mrs. S. J. Parasol, and it was raised on a fifty foot flag pole that was erected in the middle of Main Street at the intersection with Sixth Avenue. The flag pole was built in two sections so that the top part could be taken down and painted. The flag was perhaps too large and too grand for such a lowly settlement, but it flew proudly over the Ouray for many years. A band played, speeches were made, songs were sung and the day was topped off by a supper and dance. Several years later a band stand was erected about eight feet up the pole. It was handy for both political speeches and concerts. It was the beginning of a grand tradition of wonderful 4th of July celebrations which continue today.

W. H. Jackson caught these patient burros loaded down on Ouray's Main Street as they waited for a trip to the mines. Their load includes a huge blacksmith bellows, tar paper and even a stove!

In late summer of 1877 Mr. and Mrs. Dixon expanded their hotel from their log cabin to a two story log building located at the corner of Fourth Street and Sixth Avenue, which is now occupied by Ouray's Community Center. It was soon covered with more fashionable siding, and a wooden canopy extended over the plank sidewalk. The hotel's dining room was often used for dances and meetings. It was also the stop for the Barlow and Sanderson Stage which was making regular runs into the town. Later, the hotel was sold to Duran and Woodruff. The Dixon House was to serve as Ouray's premier hotel for the next ten years. The original hotel and its expansion to the west stand prominently at the center of most photographs taken at the time.

The San Juan Telephone Company and The San Juan Telegraph Company were both formed in 1878 with the purpose of bringing lines in from Lake City, Mineral Point and Silverton. However it was several more years before they were actually constructed. Western Union arrived with the railroad in 1887 and eventually put the San Juan Telegraph Company out of business. The first daily mail service began in July of 1878, and the town also began grading streets and constructing plank sidewalks. It was obvious that Ouray citizens had begun to believe that they were going to stay awhile.

For over a decade a great part of Ouray's excitement came from a newspaper and its editor. *The Solid Muldoon*, a Democratic newspaper, was first published by Dave Day on September 5, 1879 and it immediately caused a stir. In fact Colonel Frances Frakes Day was soon known nationwide for his caustic wit and bitter sarcasm, much of it very coarse for Victorian times. He relentlessly poked fun at rival towns, newspapers and people who did not agree with him, but the people ate it up and his paper was eagerly grabbed up as soon as it hit the streets. Dave Day was at one time rumored to have forty-seven libel suits against him, and his wit caused so much trouble that he was forced to carry a gun at all times.

By the end of the decade, Ouray had certainly accomplished much, but it was still a long way from becoming what truly could be called a town. The 1880 U. S. census listed 864 citizens for the town of Ouray. Eighty-eight of these souls were of school age. Eighty-five per cent of Ouray's citizens were male and all but five were white. Eighty-one per cent were native born Americans, and almost all the "foreigners" came from the British Isles. The census listed thirteen lawyers, five doctors, four clergy and three druggists. There were five saloons at the time. However Ouray's citizens knew it was still a precarious existence. Ouray's new street lights could have been snuffed out overnight, like so many mining ghost towns, by a drop in gold or silver prices or a shortage of precious minerals in the mines. The town had no volunteer fire department, no true town hall, and no courthouse. There was not a single brick building in the town. A fire could easily have wiped out half the town overnight.

W. H. Jackson caught these patient burros loaded down on Ouray's Main Street as they waited for a trip to the mines. Their load includes a huge blacksmith bellows, tar paper and even a stove!

CHAPTER THREE

Early Mining In Ouray

M ining was the reason Ouray was built and mining continued to be the main reason for its existence for over a century. However, the mining that supported Ouray was not within its city limits (even though the first recorded claim in Ouray County was so located), but rather in the steep and rugged hills that surround the town. Literally hundreds of mining claims were filed during 1875 and 1876 as swarms of prospectors flooded into the Ouray area.

The Mineral Farm Mine contained a mill and many other buildings, once it was developed. The trestle to the right led to the mine's only tunnel, as most of the ore was simply dug out of trenches.

The first major discovery was the Mineral Farm Mine, which began shipping ore soon after the arrival of A. W. Begole and John Eckles in 1875. They sold their operation to the Norfolk & Ouray Mining Company in October of 1878 for $75,000 — a tremendous sum in those days for an unimproved property. Begole demanded and received cash on the spot — no checks, cashier checks or money orders accepted by him! The Ouray Times was excited enough about the transfer to report:

> *The transfer makes an epic in the history of mining in this section and ushers in the dawn of prosperity for our people and town. Business will undoubtedly be better and money more plentiful this winter than ever before in the history of the town . . . .*

Eventually the Mineral Farm produced over a million dollars in gold, copper, lead and silver ores, but Begole and Eckles were the only owners to ever make a substantial profit from the mine. Begole wisely used his money to open a general merchandise store in Ouray. It was to become a fairly typical pattern in the years to come. The prospectors and early owners usually made a profit when they sold their rich strike, but after the mine went into full scale production and went into deeper mining, there was usually little or no profit made. There were several reasons for the losses, but seldom was it due to the value of the ore (which was usually quite high). Usually the failure to make a profit was due to expenses associated with mining the ore. Because of some very unique factors, the expenses at the Mineral Farm were much less than those of most mines in the vicinity of Ouray.

A. W. Begole and Gordon Kimball, both founders of Ouray, had stores on Ouray's Main Street. The dual wagon rig in the front was typical of freight wagons used once wagon roads had been built.

The first and foremost problem of local prospectors was the geologic makeup of the San Juans. Most local minerals were contained in fissure veins, which sometimes ran for miles. These veins occurred when the earth cracked during intense geologic activity, and the resulting space was filled with precious minerals from far within the earth. Some of these veins were less than an inch wide, and a high-grade (or valuable) vein of more than a foot or two in width was considered exceptional. Although the vein itself might be exceptionally rich, the miners needed to create a tunnel at least three feet in wide and five feet high in order to have enough room to physically continue to follow the vein. This required an awful lot of wasted effort, especially when the vein was only a few inches wide. The Mineral Farm was able to mine most of its veins in ditches, which was much less costly.

The first step in the smelting process was to crush the ore as fine as possible. This small machine finishes the job that the huge crushing mill had started. (Harper's Weekly, May 30, 1874)

Secondly the minerals in most of the San Juans were not laying loose in the ground or in exposed rows like the Mineral Farm, but rather combined in many different chemical forms and tightly bound into the hard rock of the area. Often the miners tunneled for miles underground. It usually required constant blasting, breaking and milling (basically just a process to pulverize the rock) to reduce the minerals to a form from which they could be extracted. Even then, the extraction processes were so crude and the chemical bonding of the minerals so complex that often less than half of the precious minerals were actually taken from the rock. Lead ores had to be ultimately treated by smelting. Non-lead ores could be treated by milling and amalgamation, which was a process of mixing chemicals and water with the ore and scraping the mineral laden foam from the top or bottom of the vat. The riches of the San Juans were not just laying there waiting like gold nuggets to be picked up off the ground; the extraction process was hard and costly — usually more than a single prospector-miner could ever afford to spend.

The third, and perhaps the greatest hurdle, was transportation. The San Juans are extremely rugged, and to quote George Croffut, an early travel writer, "The natural wealth of the mineral deposits in this vicinity seems to be proportional to its inaccessibility." Most of the rich mines were high up in elevation near the very tops of the mountains. It was, therefore, necessary for most ore to be shipped on the backs of burros or mules for miles to the nearest road and then possibly further by wagon or by railroads to a mill. There it could be reduced to a concentrate and shipped perhaps hundreds of miles to a smelter or an amalgamation mill for the rich minerals to be separated from the surrounding ore. For example, ore could be packed to Silverton at a cost of twenty to sixty dollars per ton (depending on the departure point and the time of year). From there it went out at additional costs over Stony Pass until 1881, when the D&RG Railroad arrived in Silverton. Another choice was to ship to the mills and smelters which were eventually built in Ouray. The concentrates could then be shipped by wagon (or by rail after the D&RG Railroad arrived in 1887) to smelters in Denver or Pueblo. Yet all of this was expensive. A good bit of the local ore was just stockpiled outside the mines until the cost of shipping could be lowered. A lot of rich ore was being mined, but it was simply too expensive to move the ore to the outside mills or smelters. As a result of high transportation costs, only $69,500 in ore was shipped from Ouray County in 1878.

After the silver or gold was reduced to a molten metal at a smelter, it would be poured into molds to make bricks for transport, some of which weighed over two hundred pounds. (Harper's Weekly, May 30, 1874)

Very few mines could afford to build a mill nearby (the Mineral Farm Mine being one of the exceptions), so men were put to work at chipping off the barren rock or low grade minerals so that only the richest ore was shipped. It was then placed in sacks and shipped to the mills at the rate of 150 to 250 pounds per burro or mule. The smelters in Ouray never proved to be very efficient, so most concentrates were shipped to smelters in Denver, Colorado Springs or Pueblo. Milling, smelting, and shipping costs always ran much more than actual mining costs, so that often the expenses of extracting and milling even rich ore were more than what the ore was worth!

One early Ouray County mine that beat costs easily was the Virginius. It was discovered at nearly 12,300 feet elevation in the Mt. Sneffles Mining District (about twelve miles southwest of Ouray) on June 28, 1876 by William B. Freeland. It started off slow, yet still averaged about $250 per ton for its ore. A dozen men worked two shafts and three tunnels that first year and the work force was increased to fifteen men the next year. It was eventually worked by a shaft down to 1,100 feet, at which time the Revenue Tunnel was driven into the mountain to tap its veins some 2,000 feet below the surface. The mine's ownership changed three times in as many years, each at a higher price, until purchased by A. W. Reynolds for $100,000 in 1880. The Virginius was extremely inaccessible, yet its ore was soon averaging eight ounces of gold and 150 ounces of silver per ton and it continued to get richer as the miners dug deeper! By 1880 Virginius ore was averaging $385 per ton.

Sometimes one wonders how the little burros could possibly carry as much weight as they did. These guys look like they have reached their limit. Burros were driven like sheep, while mules were led on ropes.

In the meantime the Wheel of Fortune Mine also continued as a major producer, sending out the largest amount of ore of any of the mines in the vicinity of Ouray. It was also rich ore — usually 250 to 300 ounces of silver per ton and sometimes three or four times that value. The mine was sold in October of 1877 to B. J. Smith and A. G. Hoyt for $160,000, but then ceased to be worked very much because of disagreements between its owners over how it should be worked.

The Yankee Boy Mine, in the basin of the same name, was staked by William Weston and George Barber in 1877 and produced $50,000 in its

This long train of mules is carrying timbers to the mines. Obviously a purchaser needed to order timbers a little longer than he expected them to be when they arrived at the mine.

The Virginius Mine was one of the highest in the world, yet its ore was very rich. Later the mine's ore was taken out from the Revenue Tunnel, which was several thousand feet lower in elevation.

first year. The next year it produced $56,000, which was a record for the Ouray area at that time. Its sorted ore was running at 103 to 396 ounces of silver per ton. In 1879, twenty three tons averaged 1,231 ounces of silver. William Weston was a graduate from the Royal School of Mines in London, and he sent out glowing reports of the area's mineral potential to mining journals all over the world. The publicity was invaluable for Ouray. His reports alone probably did more to bring mining men and capital to Ouray than any other source.

This interior shot of George Porter's store, which also served as the post office in the little settlement of Sneffles, shows the incredible array of goods that he carried for the local miners.

There were many other smaller mines in what came to be known as the Sneffles Mining District including the Hidden Treasure, the Humboldt, the Ruby Trust, the Mountain Top and the Terrible. All during the late 1870s they produced a considerable amount of the total ore that flowed into Ouray, even though their transportation costs were horrible. Every year until 1880 an attempt was made to construct a toll road to Sneffles, but it wasn't until 1880 that anything that could be considered a road reached that settlement. The "road" was totally inadequate, so in the summer of 1883, Otto Mears was called in to build a decent toll road to the Sneffles District's mines.

The small settlement of Sneffles, not to be confused with the mountain which is several miles away, had been built near the Revenue Mine. Originally it was called "Porters" after George Porter, who was a photographer, owner of the local store and also postmaster at the small settlement. The post office was started October 31, 1879, and continued until April 3, 1895. Mail was delivered to Sneffles six times a week during most of this time.

Another mining area near Ouray that proved profitable was a group of mines located along Bear Creek southeast of Ouray. Most prominent was the Grizzly Bear Mine, which was located June 16, 1875 by L. W. Balch and F. W. Sitterly. Later it was owned by George L. Wright and Milton Moore. Just over the spectacular ridge to the south were other mines that ran alongside Uncompahgre Creek. This was the original route into Ouray and several prominent mines were operated alongside what was then called Silver Hill, but which we now call the Engineer Pass jeep trail. The Silver Link, the Micky Breen, the Mother Cline and Mountain Monarch were just a few of the early day Silver Hill mines which produced large amounts of silver. They were all located in September of 1874 (a year before the settlement of Ouray) by Milton W. Cline and other prospectors. Cline went on to become Ouray's first mayor. The Mother Cline Mine, which was named after Cline's wife, was worked much like a marble quarry with big chunks of rock being taken out of the ground. The Micky Breen had a fourteen inch pay streak while the Mountain Monarch vein was two feet wide. The Royal Consort, Royal Albert and Duke of Edinburg were all claims in the Silver Hill area that followed the main vein of the Micky Breen-Monarch workings.

Many mines were also being worked in Poughkeepsie Gulch, which was named after a mine located in 1873, and produced a high grade silver-copper ore. The Poughkeepsie Mine was probably Ouray County's first mine. The Old Lout mine eventually became the biggest producer in the gulch with its production of ore worth almost a half million dollars. The Forest Mine was also a large producer. At the top of the ridge at the south end of the gulch was an area that became famous in 1879 when Leadville millionaire H. A . W. Tabor, among others, developed mines that included the Alaska and Como groups. A small settlement was established called "Poughkeepsie", which a travel writer for *Harper's Weekly* referred to as the "biggest little mining camp in the San Juans." *The Ouray Times* reported that "the excitement is intense; our streets are becoming deserted and he who cannot get a pack animal shoulders his blanket and grub and makes his way towards (Poughkeepsie)."

There were also mines along Red Canon Creek (later called Dexter Creek) to the northeast of Ouray. The Brittle Silver Mine (later called the Dexter and then the Calliope) was the most prominent. It produced ore averaging 100 ounces of silver to the ton. The Black Silver Mine was also reported to have a high grade smelting ore. Adam Herzinger located the Calliope in 1880, but Charles Nix soon had a controlling interest in many

Two prospectors or hunters, or perhaps both, have stopped before a beaver pond in Poughkeepsie Gulch. The Forest Mine is across the lake. It is easy to see from whence it got its name.

The small settlement of Portland bordered the area that Dave Day and others planned to use for the new metropolis of the San Juans - Romona. The Windham Smelter can be seen on the fill behind the town.

of the mines in the area. Even within the Ouray town limits, the Trout and Fisherman Mine continued to do well. Select ore from the mine ran as high as 1,185 ounces of silver per ton. Large shipments still averaged 394 ounces per ton.

Mr. M. Rylatt, an investor from England, and E. C. Weatherby, manager of the Chrysophie Mine, pose on October 25, 1915 in front of the Munn Brothers' Sampling Works and Assay Office.

What helped Ouray's mines the most was the passage of the Bland-Allison Act of 1878. Before 1873 the United States, as well as most of the world, had been on a bimetalist standard which established the coining of gold and silver at the standard ratio of one to sixteen. In 1873 the standard was abandoned at the same time that large quantities of silver were being found all over the western part of the United States. The results were disastrous for the mining industry. Before 1873 the price of silver had never fallen below $1.29 an ounce. After that time, the price had been continually slipping. In 1878 in an effort to help the silver mining industry, the Bland-Allison Act provided for the federal government's purchase of two to four million dollars of silver each year. For a while, this provided the needed support and the price of silver was again rising in the late 1870s.

After the passage of the Bland-Allison Act, eager speculators again began to buy and sell mining interests in the San Juans. Capital again began to flow to Ouray and new machinery could be purchased for the mines. A report of Ouray County's mines, which was made for the Windham smelter in 1878, reported:

> *Development has been slow because our mines were mainly in the hands of poor men. In 1878 not a single mine in the [Uncompahgre] district was owned by capitalists. Within the past twelve months many mines have been purchased by rich men and string companies who are able to develop their properties . . . . When one considers the manifold difficulties which have heretofore attended mining operations in thie section, he may well marvel that so many of our mines have been worked at all."*

But more money was almost always made selling stock in the mines than in taking out the ore. Many a "get rich scheme" or promise of fabulous returns on a mining investment turned out to be false. The local Ouray mines seemed to fall into one of three categories. The small operator who worked the mine himself with perhaps one or two helpers could usually turn a profit. A few of the larger mines with extremely large and rich bodies of ore (like the Camp Bird, the Revenue and the Yankee Girl) made millions and paid millions to their investors; two and three hundred per cent returns on investment were not unusual. But in between were hundreds of mines that usually couldn't be worked on any large scale at any substantial profit.

The lead engraving plate for this map was found by a friend of the author while metal detecting at Red Mountain. It is a side view of the district at the top and a bird's eye view at the bottom.

CHAPTER FOUR

A Solid Foundation

As the Town of Ouray moved into the 1880s it had grown to the second largest town in the San Juans (Silverton was the largest) and ranked in the top ten in Colorado. Yet the little settlement was still not much different than a hundred other Colorado ghost towns that one day just dried up and blew away when the rich ore in the local mountains ran out. Its community leaders were in a constant race to keep building their economic base and widen the area that they serviced. However a series of events were to occur during the 1880s and 1900s that stabilized Ouray and brought her into a period of permanence so that the bad times could be weathered. As an added benefit, it also brought culture to Ouray. The first event was the Red Mountain boom that occurred in 1882. Silver was discovered in such unprecedented amounts at Red Mountain that the district was second only to Leadville in production during the 1880s. Ouray and Silverton each lay an equal distance from the new discoveries, but time was to prove that most of the major discoveries lay on the Ouray County side of Red Mountain Pass. There was enough money coming out of the Red Mountains, (there are three of them) that it actually took both towns to fully service the mines.

A close-up view of the Yankee Girl shaft house, power plant (with the twin smoke stacks), ore house (to the left of the power house) and manager's quarters to the right.

The undisputed premier mine in the Red Mountain District was the Yankee Girl. It's tall, slender shaft house continues to stand near the center of the district as if to say that it is still king. It was the mine by which all others were measured, having produced over $8 million in ore in a little more than ten years. Some authorities believe that its total production was over $12 million. It was located August 19, 1882 and produced ore that was as rich as 3,000 ounces of silver per ton. One ten ton carload of picked and sorted ore was sold for more than $75,000. The mine was developed to 1,050 feet, but as the mine went deeper, its ore became a lower grade and operating costs became tremendous as its pumps fought to keep out large quantities of sulfuric acid and water. Otto Mears once owned an interest in the Yankee Girl and he took advantage of the opportunity to use its silver to make his world famous silver passes for the Silverton and Rio Grande Southern railroads.

The Guston Mine is located to the left with the thirty or forty buildings that made up the little settlement of Guston to the right. The tracks of the Silverton Railroad appear in the foreground.

The Genesse-Vanderbilt, to the north of the Yankee Girl, was discovered in 1882, but it developed slowly. It had a 700 foot shaft and has been worked as recently as the 1940's with exploration work done even in the 1970s. So far it has produced over a million dollars in ore. The Guston, to the south of the Yankee Girl, was located in August of 1881, before the discovery of most of Red Mountain's rich mines. It was originally operated for its lead which was needed as flux in the local smelters. It produced at least $2 1/2 million in ore with some estimates running as high as $7 million. The Robinson was also operated very closely with the Guston.

The National Belle was located right in the middle of Red Mountain Town. Its ore was found in many irregular and unpredictable caves. It was not extremely rich ore, but it was easy to mine — often it was just shoveled into sacks. The Silverton Railroad was eventually built to its front door. All this kept costs low and made it possible to mine the National Belle's low to medium grade ore at a profit. The National Belle is reported to have produced over $2 million. Visitors and tourists often came to the mine just to gawk at its "treasure caves", which were covered with crystals and glittering minerals of all shapes and colors.

Red Mountain had as much speculation occurring over its town sites as it did for its mines. In less than three years the settlements of Chattanooga, Congress, Liverpool, Guston, Red Mountain City, Hudson, Rodgersville, Ironton (also called Copper Glen), Burro Bridge, Red Mountain Town, Missouri City, Sweetville, Butte City and Del Mino were all laid out in the district. However, only Guston, Red Mountain Town and Ironton ever reached any size or lasted very long. During its hey day, there were often two or three thousand people living in the Red Mountain District in the summer.

A crew of workers is busy extending Red Mountain Town's plank sidewalks in the summer of 1891, but few of the town's residents appear at the scene. The National Belle Mine dominates the town to the left.

When the initial discoveries were made at Red Mountain, the Town of Silverton had an advantage over Ouray, as it had the best trail to the Red Mountain District. However, Otto Mears soon finished what came to be called the Million Dollar Highway into Red Mountain Town, giving the advantage back to Ouray. Then in 1888-89 Otto Mears built the Silverton Railroad into the Red Mountains. However the D&RG Railroad had come into Ouray in 1887, and it was closer to the Denver and Pueblo mills and smelters than to Silverton. So after all was said and done, each town benefited about equally from the enormous riches of Red Mountain.

The settlement of Congress was the first actually at the Red Mountain District. However the main trail through the district was relocated within a year and most of these buildings were moved to Red Mountain Town.

Many of the finest buildings of Ouray were built during the 1880s. The

impetus came mainly from the arrival of the D & RG Railroad and the Red Mountain mining boom. The town's population swelled from 864 in 1880 to 2,534 in 1890. Wages were good for the time. In March of 1885 Dave Day reported that tradesmen were paid $1 to $6 a day (depending on their exact occupation), miners $3 to $5 a day, laborers $2 to $3 and servant girls $20 to $30 per month. He reported there was "no demand

The early Million Dollar Highway was much more exciting than present. There were few places that two vehicles could pass each other, so it was sometimes necessary to back up for a half mile to let another wagon or buggy through.

for preachers, lawyers, book agents, tramps or ornamental nuisances." The Ouray officials wrote their own ordinances in 1891 and they applied to the State for official "City" status since the population had exceeded the necessary 2,000 persons. Hence the Town of Ouray became the City of Ouray — a title that it has never given up. The City of Ouray's ordinances provided some pretty practical health and safety rules for the time. It was pretty obvious that small pox and typhoid were major problems. Drivers of stages or conductors of trains were to provide the city with the name of any one suspected of small pox at least five miles before they reached town; otherwise, they were to confine the person to the conveyance until the town officials could come get them. The contents of privies could only be transported through town in closed containers except between midnight and 5 a.m. Dead animals had to be removed from town within six hours of their death.

The Circle Route Stage has just left Red Mountain Town after picking up passengers from the Silverton train. The two women on top definitely have the best seats in the house.

There were many other practical and not so practical ordinances adopted. No more than fifty pounds of blasting powder could be kept in any one place. No person could carry a pistol, derringer, dirk, dagger, slug, hand-billy or other deadly weapon in town "except for legitimate purposes." Any child under the age of sixteen could be fined if he was found in a saloon, bowling alley, billiard room, house of ill-fame or place where an obscene play was performed during the hours of 9 p.m. and 5 a.m., "unless able to give a lawful excuse therefore." Any person who employed a woman as a bartender or waiter in a liquor or beer saloon could be fined up to $100. Playing ball, flying kites or rolling hoops on the streets were all crimes. It was also illegal to ride a bicycle faster than eight m.p.h. As of 1898, children under eighteen had a 8 p.m. curfew, but the drinking age was sixteen.

Ouray's new air of permanence was due in large part to actions taken to prevent devastating fires — another reason that some of Colorado's mining camps became ghost towns over night. Ouray's first volunteer fire department was established in the early 1880s. The department's hose carts were usually pulled by men, since it took so long to hitch up the horses. Races were even held between towns to determine whose hose team was faster. A cart could easily be pulled downhill in Ouray by two men. The only problem was stopping! However it might have taken as many as ten or twelve men to pull the cart up some of Ouray's steep hills. Later a four wheel wagon was used that could be pulled by either men or horses.

The spectators are watching a hose cart race that was taking place in Telluride about the turn of the century. Ouray could well have had a team competing in this timed race.

By 1889 Ouray had two companies in its fire department — one was hook and ladder and the other a hose company. Each had its own uniform and they held separate benefit dances at the Beaumont Hotel or Wright's Opera House to raise funds — usually the Hook and Ladder Company's dance was on July 4th and the Hose Company's at Thanksgiving. At first a large circular lumber saw blade was used for the city's fire alarm, but later a big bell was placed on the steel tower that still stands behind city hall. At present the city uses sirens to call its firemen and also to announce lunchtime during the week.

A second action that helped to make the town more fire-resistant was the use of bricks in the construction of buildings. Francis P. Carney, a local contractor, turned bricks out by the tens of thousands and built many of the brick buildings in town. His brickyard was located by the present day swimming pool. Many fine and large structures were built of brick during this period including the Beaumont Hotel, the County Courthouse, City Hall and most of the larger commercial buildings in town. There were also buildings, like Wright's Opera House, which were built with brick but with steel fronts, and others, like the hospital, which were built of stone.

Francis Carney's brick plant (and resulting fish ponds) are in the foreground of this 1901 photograph. The baseball field is near the center and the railroad depot is located across the river.

The three story Beaumont was the first of the large brick buildings, having been started on July 5, 1886 and completed December 15, 1886 at a cost of $85,000. It contained forty-six sleeping rooms, was heated by steam and was one of the first of Ouray's buildings built with electricity. Most of its furnishings came from Marshall Fields in Chicago. Its grand central stairway splits half way up to each side of the second story rotundas. Its wood paneled dining room occupied over half of the second floor. Glass cases lined the lobby with samples of the richest ores from the local mines. Pictures of local scenery hung in the hallways and Navajo blankets decorated the railings and many of the hotel's easy chairs. The Circle Route stage left daily from the Beaumont for Red Mountain and Silverton. The Miners and Merchants Bank was quick to move into the first floor corner, and the Bank of Ouray occupied a spot slightly to the north. The Beaumont was originally built by a syndicate of men headed by D. C. Hartwell, which used the name the Ouray Real Estate and Building Association, but the hotel was soon rented to Col. Charles Nix, who later foreclosed on a $20,000 mortgage which he held on the building.

The Beaumont Hotel during its glory days. Some called it the prettiest hotel in all of Colorado. The Miner's and Merchant's Bank is located on the ground floor on the corner. The "ladies' entrance" was on the right.

The dining room of the Beaumont Hotel was wonderfully ornate, as shown by this photo. If the walls could only speak they could describe the many elegant social affairs held here over the years

The October 15, 1886 edition of *The Solid Muldoon* mentioned that the order of the Sisters of Mercy were taking on a hospital project in Ouray. Two weeks later they had already collected $4,000 for their project. It took only a little while longer to raise the rest of the necessary money because much of the funding came in from the larger of the nearby mines. The hospital's foundation was laid March 25, 1887 and St. Joseph's Hospital was formally opened on August 25,1887. Back in those days there was no such thing as insurance — especially for miners. Usually their unions only promised to bury them. However by paying one dollar a month to the hospital, they would be treated in the event of an emergency or sickness.

The order of the Sister's of Mercy ran St. Joseph's Hospital for many years. One of the nuns stands behind the car. The building is now used by the Ouray County Historical Society for its museum.

Ouray's school system took a major leap in 1888 when the new two story, four room brick schoolhouse was built at the northeast corner of Fourth Street and Sixth Avenue. In 1892 an identical unit was added and the old frame school building was also being used. Inside plumbing was installed at the same time. Ouray's school population was large in the 1880s and 1890s. Many of the classes contained thirty or forty students. The present building was originally built in 1937-38 but has been extensively remodeled on several occasions.

Wright's Opera House was built in 1888 by George and Ed Wright, part owners of the Wheel of Fortune Mine. The front of the building sported a magnificent Mesker's Brothers metal covering. Cast iron piers on the first floor supported an ornate pressed metal veneer on the second story. Its second story stage allowed culture to come to Ouray. The large room could hold as many as 500 people. Many locals came to call it the "Opera House", although very few operas were ever performed there. Countless other productions were put on, as well as dances and even basketball games and high school graduation ceremonies. The lower floor was originally occupied by •

the San Juan Hardware Company, which was later bought out by Arps Brothers Hardware. The local post office was also housed in the building for a while.

Ouray's large brick school house can be seen in the distance at the left, while Mother Buchanon's hot springs establishment is in the right fore-ground. Mother Buchanon also rented rooms.

The first mention of the need for a new courthouse was made in *The Solid Muldoon* in the summer of 1886, but the county didn't get around to buying lots until April of 1888. A formal ceremony was held when the cornerstone was laid in August of 1888. A large, old-fashioned courtroom still occupies most of the second floor. In modern times it was used for the courtroom scenes in "True Grit", starring John Wayne. In the 1800s the court trials themselves were the town's entertainment. Most of the original furnishings are still in the court house, as well as a fine collection of old photographs.

There were still plenty of frame buildings built in Ouray in the 1880s and 1890s, but of the large structures only the three story Western Hotel, built in 1892, has survived the ravages of fire or age. The Western originally advertised that it contained "forty three sleeping rooms, three toilets and a bath tub". It was run by Holt and Foster and served as Ouray's "working man's hotel" or the "miner's palace" for many years. The Beaumont was too expensive for miners with its rates running three and four dollars a day. Room and board at the Western ran $1.25 per day in 1899.

The same riches that helped bring permanence to Ouray also brought the seedier side of life. Although "bawdy houses" or "places for the practice of fornication" were outlawed in the 1880s, the red light district flourished along Second Street between Seventh and Eighth avenues. The Temple of

Music, Bon Ton, Bird Cage, Clipper and The Monte Carlo were just a few of the establishments' names. At the high point of the district there were over one hundred girls working the street. Pioneer of all the bawdy houses was a dance hall, saloon, and house of prostitution established in 1885 by John Vanoli and called the "220." It was located on Main Street between Seventh and Eighth and was a constant source of trouble. The block that contains today's livery stable included the Roma, the 220, the Gold Belt and a large collection of small cribs and attached rooms. The Roma was one of the rowdiest saloons in Ouray. Several people were killed there and once the killer himself was Vanoli. He went to prison for two years for killing one of his patrons but was released after only eight months in the penitentiary, when local citizens (including Dave Day) petitioned for and received a pardon from the governor. The reason? Most people in town believed his victim, Sam Best, deserved killing. It didn't matter that Vanoli shot first or that his second shot hit his victim as he was trying to lift himself off the floor.

Ouray was no longer a frontier town and had moved into a more sophisticated era by the 1890s, as shown by the ornate exterior of Albert Jeffers' store on Main Street. Note the bridal gown in the right front window.

Dance halls were also popular. The Gold Belt Theater was by far the most famous; it was located right behind the Roma and 220. For twenty-five cents a miner could dance with a girl and receive one drink. Drinks were two for twenty-five cents or fifteen cents each. Because change could not be made for two drinks for twenty five cents, tokens were used to show the customer had another drink coming. They are a favorite collectible today. The Gold Belt also presented musical and theatrical performances of a truly good quality. Even some of Ouray's social elite were attracted to their productions, which, in part, caused their wives to promote the need for an opera house.

This scene along Main Street shows the variety of businesses in Ouray. The Bucket of Blood Saloon is on the left, then a dentist, a jeweler, the Capitol saloon, City Hall, a clothier and a half dozen other establishments!

During the 1880s and 1890s Ouray was reported to have as many as thirty-five saloons, but they probably weren't all operating at the same time. Women and children were never allowed in the saloon, hence the swinging doors, so children could look under and women over to see if Dad was in the bar. Some of the saloons included the First Chance Saloon at the south end of town, and the Last Chance Saloon on the north near the present swimming pool. Later, the First and Last Chance were combined. The Bank Saloon was at the southeast corner of the Story Building. The name allowed Dad to tell Mom, "I'm going to the bank" and not lie. In defense of such inequities, Dave Day announced that "the ladies of the Episcopal Church have organized for their summer a campaign against sinners. They will devote their energies to rescuing miners and editors, as experience has taught them that lawyers and bank cashiers are not worth saving."

The Hess Saloon was at the southeast corner of Main Street and Sixth Avenue in the Hess Block, which was the first of Ouray's commercial buildings to use pressed brick. Hess' saloon was one of the few in town that didn't allow any gambling (which was actually totally prohibited by law). The Free Coinage Saloon was in the building presently occupied by the Outlaw. The Bucket of Blood Saloon, located at the northwest corner of Main Street and Fifth Avenue, was probably the most intimidating — at least in terms of the name! The Corner Saloon occupied the space now occupied by Citizen's State Bank. Manion and Beavers later bought the saloon and changed the name. The White House Saloon boasted the first stained glass windows in Ouray. The Capitol Saloon was on Main Street right next to the original City Hall. The Cabinet Saloon was founded by Tom Heibler in 1889. It was named for a large cabinet which ran across one entire wall that was filled with mineral specimens from the local mines. The Cabinet, Bucket of Blood, White House and Capitol buildings are now gone. The Ouray Brewing Company was also started in 1884. Half a gallon of beer (poured into your own container) cost twenty-five cents. The Beaumont, the Western and most of the other hotels also had a bar available in their buildings.

Events could get pretty hectic in the early saloons. This crowd even includes several dogs and three men playing the flute, fiddle and harp. At least four games of chance are depicted.

Another reason that Ouray was prospering in the 1880s was that transportation improved radically. What came to be called the Million Dollar Highway was built as a toll road to Red Mountain during 1883. When the county crews proved too slow, Otto Mears stepped in and completed it quickly. The name came from the cost of upgrading it to an automobile highway in 1924. When the road opened to Silverton in 1884, Editor Day wrote: "The ride is one that America cannot duplicate and the road the grandest and most expensive ever inaugurated and completed in the land of pluck and nerve — The Great American West." It still stands true today!

Ouray's citizens purposely built snow tunnels through the Riverside Slide, as it made a good tourist attraction. The stage was full this day, and many men and women were in the area on horseback.

Electricity came to Ouray in 1885 when Thomas Gibson and D. C. Hartwell installed a small generating plant in an annex to the Beaumont Samplings Works at the south end of Oak Street. Later, another plant was built across the river from Rice Lumber Company. Both were run by water power with an intake up the Uncompahgre. Lower water levels in the winter also made steam power necessary as a backup. Later, the intake was moved to Box Canyon, and the grade and bridges for the pipe made the inside of Box Canyon accessible to the general public for the first time. However, the tailings from the mills in the Sneffles District polluted the stream and caused abrasion problems, making it necessary to replace the water wheel every month. Therefore in 1898 the intake was moved to a dam on the Uncompahgre River just below Bear Creek Falls.

The Red Mountain to Ouray stage of about 1890 has stopped to let a photographer get off and take photographs of the awe inspiring scenery. He did it at the steepest drop off on the whole road.

In 1885 Croffut wrote, "If the miners of Ouray pray at all, it is for the coming of the 'Iron Horse'; they consider the completion of a railroad to their city, the one thing of paramount importance." In July of 1882 the D&RG had reached Silverton via Durango. In September of 1882 the D&RG also reached Montrose by the Marshall Pass route. It was tantalizing to Ouray's citizens to have railroads so close by, but it would be a few more years before the locomotive's whistle would be heard in Ouray. As early as December of 1882 Ouray business men were petitioning the D&RG to come on into town, but the D&RG was busy extending its rails into Utah and then it fell into financial trouble. All during 1885 and 1886 Dave Day called for the D&RG to bring a railroad to Ouray. A branch of the Denver and Rio Grande Railroad finally arrived in 1887, but it was a complicated path. It was originally surveyed to come in on the east side of the Uncompahgre River, but Otto Mears, Dave Day and David Moffat (president of the D&RG) decided to end the branch near the small settlement of Portland, which was four miles north of Ouray. Mears refused to give up the right of way for his toll road and George Jackson and Day formed the Chipeta Town Site Company which owned land that the railroad would have to pass through. The little town of Portland was founded in 1881(when the Utes moved out) by Preston and Enos Hotchkiss. By May of 1886 Day announced "it is morally certain that the railroad will not be built to (Ouray)." He taunted the Ouray merchants for not offering incentives to the railroad and noted "Portland is to be the metropolis of the San Juan Country."

399. Interior of Box Canyon near Ouray, Colo.

An early day tourist's post card showing the interior of Box Canyon, looking out to the east. The water line for the city's electric plant took up the major part of the walk way into the falls.

All of this did not fit well with Ouray's merchants, and they were soon boycotting Day's paper. By July, Day lashed back that, "The Muldoon never was so prosperous and crowded with job work." In the meantime the name of his proposed terminus was changed to Helena, Romona and then Chipeta. By March of 1887 Ouray citizens were ready to sell the town to get the railroad. Many of the powerful mine owners wrote Moffat demanding that he bring the railroad on into Ouray. On July 24, 1887 David Moffat arrived in Ouray, and at a meeting of its prominent citizens, offered to extend the railroad into Ouray if they would furnish and grade the right of way and buy the land for the depot (worth about $35,000). Dave Day was furious, as well as being out $6,000 of his own money. The bad feelings caused by the affair would cause Day to leave Ouray in 1892.

The first construction train arrived in Ouray on December 15, 1887. The first regular passenger train entered town on December 21, 1887. The arrival of the railroad dropped costs drastically in Ouray, and it was in great part responsible for the building boom that occurred at the same time. No other event in the history of Ouray lowered the cost of living or removed the isolation of its citizens more. Flour dropped from twenty five cents to four cents a pound. Potatoes fell from ten to one cent a pound. Freight rates for ore also dropped, although not enough or fast enough for most local citizens. When the D&RG arrived, even Dave Day had to announce:

> *The completion of such a needed and long and patiently awaited enterprise will add hundreds of thousands to our assessable wealth and enable the owners of low-grade mines that have for years been practically idle to start up and contribute their share to the permanent advancement and prosperity of the grandest of all counties in the San Juan Belt — Ouray.*

Freight is being unloaded from the D&RG's train into wagons in the foreground. This bridge leads up Seventh Avenue, and the tracks on the spur track lead to the Munn Brother's and Beaumont sampling works.

Another railroad also came to Ouray County in 1892. The Rio Grande Southern was founded by Otto Mears and ran from Ridgway to Durango via Telluride and Dolores. It had been incorporated on November 7, 1889, and construction began in 1890. The Town of Ridgway was platted May 16, 1890, and by mid-July the town was reported to have a "busy and bustling appearance." Its post office was established October 1, 1890. The town of Ridgway was founded as the terminus for the railroad and most of its life has centered around supplying the railroad or the local ranchers. It was first called Dallas Junction, then Magentie, then Ridgway Junction and finally Ridgway, after R. M. Ridgway, who was the D&RG construction superintendent and an individual who had loaned Mears a lot of the necessary equipment to build the railroad. The RGS roundhouse, yards, shops, offices and depot were located there. By 1891 Ridgway had a church, hotel, newspaper and many stores. By January 25, 1892 the RGS had been completed all the way to its other terminus in Durango. Unfortunately the new railroad would only have one good year before the Silver Crash of 1893 put it into bankruptcy.

These people are waiting for the train at Ouray's Denver and Rio Grande depot. The surrey on the right transported people up town to Ouray's hotels and restaurants.

The silver bricks that finally came out of the smelters were not light. Gold bricks were even heavier. Although the bricks weren't easy to steal, there are several security guards watching the men in this scene.

CHAPTER FIVE

Ouray's Golden Days

By the early 1890s, it was clear that Colorado's title as "The Silver State" was soon to come to an end. The price of silver was fluctuating widely. Gold had become the mistress of most mining men. In 1891 large quantities of gold were found at Cripple Creek and thereafter large amounts of capital simply could not be found for most silver mines. The repeal of the Sherman Silver Purchase Act in 1893 had a devastating effect on mining. Many of Colorado's silver camps became ghost towns overnight, leaving a wonderful legacy for today's tourist, but a horrible effect on the people of the day. Stores closed in Ouray, as well as the Bank of Ouray itself. Even Gus Begole, one of the founders of the town of Ouray, went out of business — even though he had reportedly been doing $200,000 a year in sales. Many men roamed the streets looking for work.

The Fourth of July parade in 1893 was a well attended affair. Note the huge flag still hangs on the flagpole in the center of Main Street. A. W. Begole's store is to the left of center.

Times were so tough that on July 29, 1893, the Ouray City Council voted to turn off the electric street lights after the electric company refused to discount their rates because of the hard times. Now the town literally seemed to have a dark future. The lights remained off for over a year and were only partially relit at that time. The city also reduced the salaries of municipal employees by twenty per cent, stopped sprinkling water on the streets to keep the dust down and allowed businesses to spread out their license fees over a period of time. In the November 1896 presidential election, the question of silver's prominence came to a head when William Jennings Bryan pledged a return to the bimetalist standard. Ouray voted a hundred to one for Bryan, but it didn't prevent defeat.

However Ouray, although hit hard, was spared the fate of becoming a ghost town due to several factors. One was the discovery of gold in the late 1880s at what became known as Gold Hill or the Gold Belt directly northeast of town. By early 1889, the Gold Belt mines were well established. By March 8, 1889, the front page of *The Solid Muldoon* proclaimed, "Gold by the Bucketful from the Gold Belt." One of the most promising of the mines was the American Nettie which was actually made up of two claims — the American and the Nettie. The American was located on October 8, 1885, by John Porter and Thomas Nash. The Nettie and the Schofield were located in November of 1888, by W. P Barringer and W. P. Conner. The group was sold for $43,000 on March 21, 1889.

The American Nettie Mine hangs high on the cliffs to the northeast of Ouray. A rough, steep trail led from the city to the mine, yet many of its miners chose to live in Ouray and make the hike daily.

The claims eventually spread all over the mountain to the northeast of Ouray. Tom Walsh, recognizing the value, worked the dumps at the American Nettie in 1896. The American Nettie was one of the area's first mines to use electricity. It continued to operate profitably, eventually containing over sixteen miles of underground workings and producing over $2 million in ore. A tram connected the mine to its mill across the Uncompahgre Valley, and the miners could often be seen going up or coming down in one of the tram's two ore buckets. The tram worked off gravity — a bucket of ore going down pulled the other bucket up. The tram was known as one of the highest in the world, as the American Nettie Mine was 1800 feet higher than its mill on the valley floor. Unfortunately, an airplane hit its cable in the 1960s and it was taken down.

The Bachelor Mine was at the high point of its existence in 1900 and the small settlement of Ash had grown up in the area. The road behind the mine led up to the Wedge Mine.

The Bachelor Mine came into prominence in 1890, but its fabulously rich vein was not discovered until 1892. The mine was located at the end of Dexter Creek Canyon across from the Calliope Mine. For a while, it reportedly produced $30,000 a month. The Bachelor eventually totaled high grade silver ore in excess of $3 million. A settlement and post office, named "Ash," was established at the location. The town derived its name from the last names of the three bachelors who owned the mine at the time (Armstrong, Sanders and Hurlburt). Higher up on the same mountain were the Wedge and the Neodesha mines. The Wedge was extremely rich, producing $2 million in ore, some of which ran as high as 15,000 ounces of silver (50% silver). The settlement of Ash eventually contained almost three hundred people. C. W. Comforth and Son made daily trips from Ash to Ouray carrying mail and supplies in their wagon, which was pulled by a four horse team. Later on the Bachelor and Wedge veins were worked out of the Syracuse Tunnel near Lake Lenore. Close by lay other good producers — among them, the Pony Express, the Sieburg and the Wanakah mines.

Even with the arrival of the railroad in Ouray in 1887, there was still a need for packers to bring the rich ore down from the high mountain mines. Teamsters (if they used horses) or muleskinners (if they drove mules) were some of the hardest working, best paid and most highly respected men in town. Their work day would usually start at five a.m. and ended long after dark. One of the best freighters in the 1890s and early 1900s was John Ashenfelter, who maintained a barn on Second Street in Ouray, as well as at the Camp Bird and Revenue mines. At one time he kept over fifty wagon teams (called "big sixes" for the six huge draft horses that pulled them), one hundred burros and fifty pack mules on the trail.

For many years, Dave Wood carried freight from the D&RG terminus in Montrose to Ouray and on to Red Mountain or even Silverton. The eight mules could easily pull two wagons, but the trip took five days round trip.

He also kept about fifty horses available for rent. Miners would rent the horses in town, take them to the mines, tie the reins to the saddle horn and let the animals walk back down. The horses learned quickly, and it was quite a familiar sight to see a riderless horse headed back down the mountain trails to Ashenfelter's barn. A typical freight team had three or four pairs of mules or horses pulling it; the freight wagons of the time had extremely large wheels and could carry five or six tons of ore. Heavy brakes were necessary, and they were attached to long poles for leverage. Pack mules were usually tied together and led in long strings. Burros were usually driven like sheep. All of this also required a massive support system for feed, health care, shoeing and keeping up the corrals. Ashenfelter kept forty men working just at his Ouray barn; his teams packed an unbelievable amount of Camp Bird and Revenue ore in terms of both weight and value. He died in 1902, and his business was then sold to John McDonald who was also a well respected freighter.

Dave Wood was another famous early freighter. He operated all over Colorado, but in later life he settled down to mainly hauling freight between the towns of Gunnison, Montrose, Ouray and Telluride during the time period before the railroad came to those towns. He brought in goods from the outside world and took out the ore that he, Ashenfelter and others had brought down from the high mountain mines. Wood advertised himself as the "largest freighting outfit in the West" — and he may well have been. His short cut route from Montrose to Telluride across the Uncompahgre Plateau is now a jeep road that carries his name.

A lumber and provision burro train was fighting its way through deep snows in the vicinity of Ouray. The burros had to stay on the trail or they would flounder. (Harper's Weekly, June 9, 1883)

There was still plenty of ore for Ashenfelter and Wood to haul — even after the Silver Panic of 1893. The Revenue Tunnel was completed in 1893 at a cost of $600,000. Prime developer was A. E. Reynolds who was backed financially by the Thatcher brothers. The tunnel cost a lot of money, but it allowed the Virginius to be tapped at a much lower level, which in turn allowed very profitable operations for many years to come. As the price of silver fell, the Revenue simply produced more of it at cheaper costs. As an added benefit, more and more gold showed up in the Revenue ore as the mining went deeper.

The Revenue was one of the first mines in the world to use electricity, although it was dangerous direct current which carried 500 volts. As a result, several miners and animals were killed in the mine. Electricity was such a new invention that one of the miners in 1896, despite being warned repeatedly, reached behind a safety guard and touched a bare wire "to see what it would feel like." No one will ever know as the incident resulted in his immediate death. There were no electrical switches at the Revenue boarding house. The men simply unscrewed the light bulb or covered it with a can if they wished to sleep. Besides lighting, electricity was eventually used for the small locomotives that powered the ore trains and for the machinery in the Revenue Mill.

The Revenue's huge mill is located at the center of the photo, while Ashenfelter's barns are at the right. The buildings at the right are Porter's store and the post office for the settlement of Sneffles.

Snow slide victims have been brought down in sleds to the little settlement of Sneffles before going on to Ouray. Life in the mountains was extremely dangerous in the winter.

As many as six hundred men were employed at the Revenue Mine during this period and the little settlement of Sneffles prospered. The Revenue built a huge, sixty stamp mill that could process five hundred tons of ore a day. In terms of men, the Revenue Mine became even larger than the Camp Bird. The two together were by far the largest employers in the county. The 1900 census listed 442 men living and working in the Sneffles area.

Another factor that saved Ouray from a fate like Aspen or Creede (which were purely silver towns) was the fact that many of the Ouray mines had always carried at least a small percentage of gold. In silver's heyday it was sometimes easy to overlook an ounce or two of gold when it was combined with 300 or 400 ounces of silver. In fact, at one time the local mills and smelters didn't even pay for less than a half ounce of gold.

Now the gold became important. Even small amounts could keep the mines operating. Most of the Red Mountain mines also started producing a larger percentage of gold as they went deeper. By 1895 after the initial panic subsided, the Ouray economy began to recover. One thing that continued to help all of the local mines was the railroad. It meant a much lower grade ore could be shipped at a profit or the same grade ore could be shipped at much less cost. The use of electricity and pneumatic drills further dropped costs. At the end of the nineteenth century, the Revenue and Camp Bird mines sent out a steady stream of silver and gold concentrates, and the American Nettie was near its high point in production.

Tom Walsh was a very dignified man, and he never forgot that he once was a "working man." Even after he was worth millions, he championed the causes of the common man.

The event that secured Ouray's future came in 1896, when Tom Walsh discovered the Camp Bird mine. Before that time, Walsh had some mining success in Rico, Cripple Creek and Leadville, but the 1893 Silver Panic put him on the verge of bankruptcy. In 1896 he was the manager of a smelter treating Red Mountain ores in Silverton and times were tight. Walsh needed lead ores that could be used as flux for his smelter. Eventually Walsh and his old friend, Andy Richardson, ended up looking at a few of Andy's claims in Imogene Basin. Walsh acquired the Hidden Treasure mine and later spent the time to look at the neighboring Gertrude, a valuable mine which had been sold earlier to its present owners for $50,000. When Walsh assayed ore from the mine, he discovered that it contained a form of Telluride gold that ran as high as $3,000 per ton. He immediately purchased the Gertrude and its adjoining claims, and he also started staking additional claims in the area. The first new claim was called the Camp Bird after the blue jays or camp robber birds that frequented the area. By 1900 Walsh had accumulated 103 claims covering some 900 acres.

This is only a small part of the men that worked at the Upper Camp Bird Mine in 1904. There were just as many men working in the mill below. The men were all well dressed and looked happy — typical of the Camp Bird.

Walsh did such a good job of keeping his work secret, that before the people of Ouray even knew what was going on, Walsh was already milling the dumps at the Camp Bird. This provided him with instant capital to continue his work. Within five years, he had made over four million dollars. By 1900 he had also spent over half a million dollars on surface improvements to the mine — much of which was spent for comforts for his four hundred miners, who now worked eight hour shifts instead of the usual ten. After 1898 they lived in considerable comfort in several three story boarding houses near the Camp Bird's upper workings at 11,200 feet elevation. The miners' quarters contained electric lights, pool tables, steam heat, hot and cold running water, reading rooms with current magazines, literature and newspapers of the day, porcelain bath tubs with indoor plumbing, fire protection devices, hardwood floors, first-aid stations and even marble counter tops for the lavatories. The miners ate off porcelain dishes in the dining room instead of the usual tin plates. The boarding house also served as a local hotel and restaurant, feeding fifteen to fifty travelers a day free meals and giving them a place to sleep. Other mines in the area charged twenty-five to thirty-five cents a meal.

The Ouray Teamster and Packer's Union's Fourth of July float stopped in front of the Munn Brothers' Assay Office and Sampling Works. Note the street light hanging in the middle of the street.

Conditions were good enough at the Camp Bird and the Revenue, that even though major labor troubles were occurring all over the San Juans at this time, there were no major problems at either of the mines. Even after

Walsh had sold the Camp Bird Mine, he pushed for fair treatment of all miners. In his 1908 Colorado School of Mines commencement address, Walsh urged the future mining engineers and owners to treat miners "with humanity and justice" and provide plenty of good food, clothing and medical attention. He felt strongly that by reasoning and listening to the men, labor strikes could almost always be averted.

The miners often traveled in the Camp Bird's ore buckets which ran on a tram for two miles from the mine to the mill, even though it was technically illegal. However, they didn't usually hold hands!

Walsh eventually built a large mill near the entrance to Imogene Basin, which was at a much lower elevation. It was connected by a two mile tram to the upper workings. The sixty stamp mill was fed some two hundred tons of ore a day and in turn produced about ten tons (worth $5,000 to $6,000) in gold concentrates. Armed guards brought the day's production to Ouray each day. In 1902 the Camp Bird Mine was sold for $5,200,000 to a British syndicate which continued to operate it until 1911. By the time the syndicate stopped work on the mine, it had produced a total of over twenty-six million dollars in ore (of which over sixteen million was profit). The mine grew to the point that it had its own post office at the upper workings from April 28, 1898 to March, 1918. It also had its own dairy and several stores at the mill. Eventually over a ninety year period, the Camp Bird would produce over $50 million.

Even with the large number of workers at the Camp Bird and the Revenue mines, the population of the City of Ouray was decreasing — dropping to 2,196 in 1900. One thing that didn't help matters was the influx into Ouray of influenza, typhoid fever and the small pox during the 1890s. However Ouray was not hit nearly as hard as Silverton which in one year lost almost half of its citizens.

Even though the population was decreasing, the city fathers needed a new jail. The old one still "leaked" and there was still a "wild" element in town. For example in 1895 Vanoli shot another customer in the Gold Belt Theater. Even though the victim was shot three times (one of which was in the back as he was fleeing), no charges were ever brought. However the citizens of Ouray did start a movement to try to close down all dance halls, gambling establishments and bawdy houses as well as demanding that saloons should close at midnight and on Sundays. All of the establishments stayed open for the time being, but Vanoli killed himself with a gun shot to the head about six months later.

The Camp Bird's mill was an enormous structure, and it was surrounded by many assay offices, work shops and storage facilities on the left. To the right are the miners' boarding houses, as well as houses for supervisors and their families.

The city council explored the idea of including a new jail as part of a one story, brick city hall. When Tom Walsh heard about the new construction he was anxious to contribute his part to the effort. The new city hall was already under construction by Kullerstrand and Reynolds in 1900 when Walsh offered to pay for a second floor which would contain a gym and a library. The gym equipment never materialized, but the library was completed in 1902, and the gym space was made into a nice reading room.

Walsh actually lived in Ouray for only a few years, but in that time he endeared himself to the locals. He often held parties or balls and invited the entire town. Not only did he build the library, but he furnished it by purchasing several private libraries (containing 6,589 volumes) and art collections. Walsh also gave the library new tables, chairs, bookcases and. $2,500 to start a fund to buy new books. All of his gifts to the library

The original City Hall and Walsh Library was a replica of Independence Hall. It was destroyed by fire in 1950 but recently rebuilt to look much (but not quite) like the original.

together totaled over $30,000. So grand was the library's gala opening, that even the governor of Colorado and his wife attended. Walsh felt called to publish an apology in the local paper to the many Ouray citizens who couldn't attend the opening — the small amount of room would simply not allow him to invite everyone. Even with such wealth, it never went to Walsh's head. However his daughter, Evalyn, went on to join up with high society when she married Edward McLean, publisher of the Washington Post and a millionaire in his own right. They eventually bought the Hope diamond, but after her life turned for the worse, she felt sure the diamond was cursed and gave it to the Smithsonian Museum.

This scene is unlikely, as it was considered very unlucky for women to be underground in a mine. The two are not in their working clothes, but the two men don't seem to mind.

In 1896 the Revenue was as large, if not as profitable, as the Camp Bird with over five hundred men turning out a high grade ore. By 1903 it had three electric plants supplying power to the mine. One of them was even located in far off Ouray. The Revenue Tunnel allowed the miners to work the Humboldt, Atlas, Governor, Monarch, Terrible, Bimetalist and the Virginius as well as many other veins. By 1912 the Revenue had produced over $15,000,000 in ore. It was sending out forty or fifty tons of concentrates a day, but dollar wise it wasn't keeping up with the Camp Bird ore, which contained a lot more gold.

Burros (at the left) and mules (at the right) are waiting to be loaded with ore sacks at the Revenue Mine at Sneffles, Colorado. At least this many animals were needed for each day's shipments.

The road from the Revenue and Camp Bird mines was packed daily by almost a hundred wagons pulled by six huge draft horses, as well as several pack teams of mules and several hundred burros — all making their way to Ouray. Two stages made daily trips from Ouray to Sneffles. Brown's dairy wagon also made the trip daily to deliver a hundred and fifty gallons of milk and cream to the mines. There was also a considerable tourist trade; each summer thousands of visitors rode, drove or walked up the mountain road to view the scenery and see the famous Camp Bird and Revenue mines.

Even though Ouray's population was decreasing, the St. Elmo Hotel was built by Kittie Heit, just to the south of her Bon Ton Restaurant in 1898. Kittie was married to Joe Heit and she had bought the restaurant in 1890. Evidently Kittie made all of the couple's business decisions. The St. Elmo is a solid brick building while the restaurant was frame. Today's Bon Ton patio is where the restaurant stood. Mrs. Heit had cooked and run her restaurant from 5 a.m. to 12 midnight seven days a week to raise the money to build the hotel. A popular diversion was to eat at her establishment and then attend the concerts at the Wright Opera House next door. The St. Elmo is still remarkably preserved.

The Elks' Club building is still under construction in the summer of 1905 when this photo was taken. The small bridge on Main Street in the foreground funneled traffic down to one lane.

Many of Ouray's beautiful Victorian homes were built during the period of the late 1890s. A few good examples are the W. A. Reynolds house at 510 Fifth Avenue (built in 1895), the Dr. W. W. Ashley house at 505 Fourth Street (built in 1891), the George Hurlburt house at 432 Fourth Street (extensively rebuilt in 1894), the Tanner home at 4th St. and 3rd Avenue (built in 1896), the William Story house at 342 Seventh Avenue (built in 1895), and the Louis King home built at 325 Seventh Avenue (built in the mid-1880s.)

The Elks Club building was built in 1904 and its formal opening was held June 6, 1905. It is a combination of French, Queen Anne and Romanesque architecture. Ouray Lodge No. 492 was the first on the Western Slope having been organized in 1898, with Dr. W. W. Rowan serving as the first Exhaulted Ruler. The interior contains many of its original furnishings including several inoperable slot machines, a beautiful pressed metal ceiling and a bar that was brought down from one of the Ironton saloons.

The dotted line was suppose to be the line of the Joker Tunnel as shown in its prospectus. However the tunnel actually ran in a different direction. Nevertheless, this photo was used because it showed most of the existing mines.

Red Mountain's Joker Tunnel was finished in 1906. It was built to solve many of the problems that plagued the great Red Mountains mines — the Guston, Yankee Girl, Robinson and Genessee-Vanderbilt. By coming in under the lower workings, it allowed ore cars to carry the ore out by gravity instead of expensive hoisting, and water to flow out naturally without the need for pumping. By 1907 about thirty five men were working in the tunnel and the idea worked! Water levels were immediately lowered and workings that no one had been able to get to for years were accessible. Intense mining began immediately, but unfortunately the ore continued to be of a middle to lower grade. The Joker Tunnel was worked off and on until it finally was abandoned altogether in the 1940s.

The Barstow Mine was also very active at this time. It was originally called the Bobtail Mine and is located in the western edge of the Red Mountain District, although its vein is much more typical of what is found in the Telluride District. Top production was between 1895 and 1918. It produced small pockets of extremely rich "gray copper" (which actually has little or no copper), but most of its ore was of a lower grade nature. For quite some time, near the turn of the century, it was the only mine operating in the Red Mountain District. It produced a total of slightly less than a million dollars in ore, chiefly in gold, silver, base metals and fluorite during World War I. The Barstow had its own mill with a tram bringing ore from the mine. Serious operations stopped after World War I, but the Barstow's ore was later worked successfully underground by the Idarado.

At the turn of the century, Ouray was beginning to look like a true city. Originally all of the trees in the valley had been cut down for cabins, fuel or lumber. Now the new growth was maturing, just like the town.

CHAPTER SIX

Into The Present

T he early 1900s were a time of deteriorating metal prices, enhanced only by a temporary rise in values during World War I. As a result Ouray's population slid from 2,196 in 1900 to only 1,165 in 1920. Even the great Camp Bird and Revenue mines were in trouble, on occasion operating with only skeleton crews. In 1906 an avalanche and resulting fire destroyed the Camp Bird mill, but since the mine was doing well at the time, a newer and larger model was built. In the hope of lowering costs, the 14th level adit (tunnel) was driven in 1918 from the mill site to the upper workings. It provided ventilation, drainage and made the tramway unnecessary. Later in 1928, a small company called the King Lease was successfully formed to operate the Camp Bird. Although the value of its ore had dropped, the mine still shipped significant amounts of silver, lead, copper, zinc and gold. During the next thirty years it would extract another $20 million in ore, but its heyday was over.

The settlement of Ouray was losing its capability to continue to prosper solely as a mining town. If Ouray had been located in another spot, it might

Ouray's railroad yard was impressive in the 1890s. The depot is to the right and freight and section buildings to the left. The second bridge over the river (next to the depot) led straight up Eighth Avenue to the red light district.

have just disappeared altogether, but more and more people began to realize that its natural setting could be just as valuable as the ore still locked in the veins that surrounded the town. In order to attract tourists, Ouray needed a more "civilized" atmosphere. The change began in 1902 when *The Ouray Herald* applauded the closing of Ouray's dance halls. It was noted that the tourists had to walk through the seedy area of town when passing from the depot to the hotels near the center of town. The editor reported that:

> (T)his marks the beginning of a new and more progressive era in the social conditions of Ouray.... Dance halls are the product of new mining camps in the mountains and boom camps on the border of civilization and Ouray has long outlived the excuse for such institutions, if indeed, there ever was one.

When the dance halls closed the neighboring towns complained that many of the proprietors moved operations to their towns.

In 1903 slot machines and most gambling were outlawed in Ouray. The saloons and houses of prostitution stayed open for the present. Ouray officials now billed the city as "the most picturesque town in the world." The Circle Trip, which was made from Ouray to Silverton by stage and then by railroad to Durango and Ridgway, was extremely popular. The stage itself had became a tourist attraction since it was a bygone relic in most parts of the country. The large amount of snow that built up at the Riverside slide on the Million Dollar Highway was another attraction. The locals purposely tried to dig a tunnel through the snow each spring, rather than just clear the road. It was always a sad day in July or August when the roof of the tunnel collapsed.

Perhaps the state of affairs in Ouray was best epitomized by Alfred Castner King, a miner who, after he was blinded by an explosion in the Bachelor Mine, began to write about the beauty of the San Juans as he remembered them. He wrote two books, *The Passing of the Storm* and *Mountain Idylls and Other Poems*, but he is best remembered for traveling all of the United States to recite his poetry from memory — even though some of his poems ran for fifty pages! His 1907 dedication to the second book marked what was happening: "To a rapidly disappearing class, the pioneer prospectors, whose bravery, intelligence and industry blazed the trails in the western wilderness for advancing civilization . . . ." King stretched across two eras. Now it was time for the tourist, the poet or the artist to descend on Ouray.

Ouray's natural attractions were obvious; even the earliest prospectors never failed to comment on Ouray's beauty. As early as July of 1877 *The Ouray Times* touted Ouray's beauty to the outside world while emphasizing the value of its mines. Even William's *1877 Tourist Guide to the San Juan Mountains,* which was actually a prospector's guide, acclaimed Ouray's picturesque location. As soon as the D&RG Railroad arrived in Ouray, it began promotion of its charms unceasingly — "For health, wealth and the grandest scenery on earth, visit OURAY." The railroad pushed the hot springs; it praised the fishing and game in the area, it extolled the mines and mentioned the pure, cold streams in the vicinity. The Circle Route brochure even proclaimed that if the tourists were lucky enough, they might see a grizzled, old prospector alongside the road leading a pack train of burros. In 1889 *The Solid Muldoon* estimated that 10,000 Circle Route tourists would visit the town that summer.

The amphitheater has always been the crown of the City of Ouray. It is especially beautiful when the clouds hand low over the town, as shown in this photo taken about the turn of the century.

After the Silver Crash of 1893, C. L. Hall wrote a mining journal of Ouray County, but he also was enchanted with its beauty. "Ouray is peerless. She will be famous as a mountain resort when many of the now famous watering places are abandoned and forgotten." Now, instead of promoting its mineral wealth, it was time for Ouray's beauty to be recognized, while still noting that untold millions in ore were left in the mountains. Mining never died completely, but the business emphasis of Ouray was changing steadily.

The interior of Dr. Rowan's drug store near the turn of the century reveals what might be the key to the city over the post office's general delivery window in the rear of the store.

Box Canyon Falls had been used as a local tourist attraction since Ouray's early days. Geologists estimate that the "sculpturing" that produced the falls required over 1,750,000 years. Box Canyon Falls encompasses the Trout and Fisherman lodes — discovered along with the town site in 1875. Edward McIntire bought the two claims from Whitlock and Staley soon thereafter. The city leased the land for a park until McIntyre's death in 1920, at which time the property was purchased for seventy-five dollars. From the time of Ouray's discovery, people would wade up Canyon Creek to see the falls, but it was a task taken by only the most adventurous. After Ouray's electric plant was built, the tourists could walk up the wooden floor that supported the pipeline. About 1898, what came to be called the "high bridge" was built to carry water from the city's two reservoirs A walk along the high bridge became a popular but dangerous way to see the falls. In the early 1900s the city started fixing up the Box Canyon area as an actual park with picnic tables, drinking fountains, lights and parking.

Ouray's local wildlife was also especially attractive to the tourists. In the winter of 1907-08 the local big horn sheep were desperate for food, and eventually some of the rams came down by the railroad depot and were fed hay. Over the years, more and more sheep appeared at the depot until almost a hundred showed up each winter. Feeding time was usually right before the train's departure so that the tourists could see the sheep. There are still a few bighorns in the Ouray area but not nearly as many as in the past. One extremely old ram even hung around the ball park every winter in the early 1990s. Sometimes he would even walk the city streets. One winter it simply failed to appear and was later found dead of old age.

This post card shows lower Box Canyon, as well as the high bridge which was constructed at the park. The card notes that the weather has been rainy and cold, although it was postmarked June 6th.

In 1920 the Ouray Recreational Association was formed as an independent part of the local Elks Club, with the stated purpose of establishing a game preserve and resort on a large scale at Ouray. Elk were brought in and released in the local mountains, and since there was no hunting season, the herd grew quickly. The elk would often walk into town and graze at the park or alongside Main Street. In the winter of 1938 four large bulls became the town pets and for the next three or four years they came back, sometimes joined by others. It was at this time that Ouray's famous photographs of elk in front of the Elks' Club were taken. Elk can still be seen in the vicinity of Ouray, but they seldom come into town. Deer, however, can usually be seen on Ouray's streets almost every day of the winter.

In 1914 a petition was circulated and money was obtained to buy land for the city to use as a playground and park. A citizens' committee soon zeroed in on the old baseball field at the north end of town. The northeastern end had also been used by Francis Carney for making bricks in the 1880s and 90s, and the goldfish that had been released into the resulting pits were thriving in the hot water. No one really took care of them, but they reproduced and grew quite large. For many years, the area had been referred to merely as "the fish ponds." In the late 1910s the town did extensive cleanup and landscaping at the park. A fountain was built in the middle of one of the ponds, a gazebo constructed nearby and a picnic area established. In 1921 Ed Washington, a local saloon keeper, brought a two foot alligator from Louisiana to add to the pools. When the animal began to wander, a small iron fence was built around one of the ponds. The alligator bellowed so much that it was determined it was lonesome and another alligator was obtained to keep the first company. Both eventually grew to be over six feet long!

Many of Ouray's hot springs have been put to private use over the years. In July of 1879, W. J. Buchanon built a small indoor pool supplied with hot water from near the present day Wiesbaden. The sides and bottom were lined with boards and the overflow ran all the way down 6th Avenue into the Uncompahgre River. By the 1890s it had become known as "Mother Buchanon's Bath House." Later in the 1920s, Dr. C. V. Bates took over the Sister's of Mercy Hospital and also ran the Buchanon hot caves in connection with his sanitarium. He claimed the cave's waters carried the highest percentage of radioactivity in the world! He felt particularly equipped to help patients with rheumatism or kidney disorders. His patients were also encouraged to drink mineral water that ran from springs up on the hillside, as it was touted to cure a variety of ailments.

In 1890 A. G. "Doc" Dunbar built a two story bath house on the corner of Second Street and Sixth Avenue. It was filled with the overflow from Buchanon's operation. It was called the Dunbarton, and its pool was much larger than Buchanon's. It also had individual bath tubs that could be rented for twenty-five cents each. Dunbar claimed his water cured rheumatism and blood disease. The pool area was popular with both locals and tourists and was lined with a wonderful sea shell collection from around the world.

Another factor that encouraged tourism was the passage of the federal "Good Roads Bill" in 1916. For the first time, large amounts of federal money were made available for local roads. During 1921 to 1924, some of those

Ed Washington's alligators' were enjoying the hot water at the fish ponds (by the present day swimming pool) on this pleasant day in the mid-1920s. The fenced enclosure kept the animals from wandering.

In the 1920s, C. V. Bates ran his "Radium Vapor Health Institute at the present day location of the Wiesbaden. The sign also advertised that "electric treatments" were available at his establishment!

funds were used locally to convert the Million Dollar Highway from a wagon road to one that could be used by automobiles. With the appearance of the automobile and then the building of decent roads, there was much more freedom for people to move about throughout the United States, and the tourist industry immediately boomed throughout the San Juans.

These early day tourists have stopped to enjoy the views on the newly upgraded Million Dollar Highway in the mid -1920s. The location is close to today's Riverside Slide snowshed.

Perhaps the end to what could be called Ouray's "Good Old Days" officially came in 1916 when Colorado voted to go dry. The San Juans, in true pioneer fashion, had voted to stay wet but were overridden by the rest of the state. Some of the local (and still illegal) bawdy houses stayed, but many of the women moved on to "better pickings" or married local men. Colorado's dry vote was followed by the Eighteenth Amendment to the United States Constitution in 1919. The few saloons and bawdy houses that still remained soon disappeared, but enterprising and energetic Ourayites changed the local emphasis to bootlegging liquor. It was almost impossible for the authorities to find liquor distilling operations in the rugged San Juans and the bootleggers prospered. Indications of just how prevalent the practice was can be found in the names of several local landmarks (such as Moonshine Park) and in the number of hidden stills that have been found when older homes have been torn down or have undergone restoration.

Bootlegged booze is being destroyed at the corner of Sixth Avenue and Main Street in 1916. It was almost $700 worth of liquor and the first destroyed in Ouray after Colorado became a dry state on January 1st.

In the 1920s Ouray's citizens took decisive action to assure that the city would become a tourist resort. For years there had been talk of a large municipal swimming pool, and in 1923 the Ouray Recreational Association began the task of raising the necessary money. Citizens contributed anywhere from $5 to $100 each, and during the next two years the 150 by 280 foot pool was built. It ranges in depth from two feet to ten feet and is so large that it takes over a million gallons of hot water to fill it. It was always suspected that a large amount of hot water was located just below the park as the grass stayed green most of the winter. The constantly melting snow caused problems for local freighters who were using sleds everywhere else in the winter. So certain was the existence of large amounts of hot water, that no attempt was even made to look for it until after the pool was built. Unfortunately an extensive search produced only a small trickle of hot water. Recently wells have been drilled at the site and enough hot water was found, but it was at a depth of several hundred feet.

For over a year the pool stood empty for lack of water, but Ouray's citizens held fund raisers and volunteered their labor to build a mile long pipeline from a hot spring at Box Canyon. By late 1927 the pool finally opened. Ten cabanas with wooden sides and canvas tops were built for bathers to change clothes and the pool was in business.

The brand new swimming pool and fish ponds were Ouray's pride in 1927. The changing cabins, to the left of the pool, were later washed down the river in the flood of 1929.

Unfortunately the stock market crash was not the only trouble that Ouray encountered in 1929. A flash flood caused both the Uncompahgre River and Skyrocket Creek to overflow their banks, bringing tons of debris and water that filled the pool and washed away the cabanas. The gold fish and the alligators also disappeared into the flood waters. Money was very tight, but the next spring volunteers dug out the debris and finished the bath house that had been started shortly before the stock market crash. In spite of its efforts, the Ouray Recreation Association eventually gave up on the pool and deeded the project to the City of Ouray, which in turn leased the premises to various private individuals. The pool was immediately a great hit and made a good profit even during the depression. It was at that time that the WPA re-channeled the Uncompahgre River and expanded the ball field near the pool.

The alligators were now gone and gradually the gold fish ponds were reduced to their present size. The city took over management of the pool and widely advertised it as "the most radioactive on the American continent" — a grossly exaggerated claim, but one that drew many visitors at a time when radioactivity was felt to be beneficial. The railroad brought people regularly from as far as Telluride, Montrose and Grand Junction, and they were encouraged to drink the water for cures of arthritis, rheumatism and many other ills. The pool area was recently remodeled and still is the focus of Ouray's wintertime economy.

The swimming pool is being "mucked out" by volunteers after the flood of 1929. The D&RG locomotive is being turned around on the man powered turntable in the background.

In 1950 a fire of undetermined origin burned Ouray's city hall and library building to the ground. The priceless library books, art work and mineral specimens (then valued at $300,000) were totally destroyed. The building was rebuilt at the time as best as the citizens could afford, but in 1990 it was restored to look very much like the original miniature Independence Hall facade. The railroad depot also burned about the same time, but, other than the historical loss, it really didn't matter since the last regular passenger service train had left Ouray on September 14, 1930. The last train of any type ran on March 21, 1953, at which time the rails were pulled back to Ridgway. The Ridgway rails, in turn, were pulled to Montrose in the late 1970s.

During and following World War II, there was a dramatic increase in local mining production. The Revenue was reworked and operated off and on right up to present; large amounts of ore are still in its ore stopes just waiting for metal prices to rise. The Camp Bird and the Idarado were also

A Rio Grande Southern excursion train is getting ready to leave Ouray. Probably visitors from Telluride have came over for a baseball game or to swim in the pool. The hotels' bus is parked against the station.

The Western Hotel in 1942 is showing the effects of decades of hard times in Ouray. The front badly needs repairing and painting. The Western has been reconditioned and still operates today.

operated very profitably during the war. A great deal of Ouray's "historical artifacts" were gobbled up during World War II as every loose piece of metal that could be found was shipped off to help the war effort. This included mill equipment, boilers, ore cars and even railroad tracks.

The Idarado Mine was a mainstay of the local work force from the 1930s on up into the 1970s. Many informed people will tell you that there are still millions to be taken out of the mine.

The Idarado mine, which is located directly alongside Highway 550 near the top of Red Mountain, was worked steadily until the late 1970s. It represents a collection of mines stretching all the way from Red Mountain to Telluride. Its interconnected workings total over ninety miles! The Idarado's portal was originally located as the Treasury Tunnel in 1896. In the early 1900s, a spur was run to the mine from the main track of the Silverton Railroad. In 1954 a fire destroyed a large portion of the Idarado's surface buildings, but the company rebuilt. Many of the little houses near the mine were brought in from the ghost town of Eureka. Eventually the Idarado Mine was extended all the way through the mountain to Telluride, although near the middle, it is necessary to descend over a thousand feet down a shaft. Geologists still claim that there are plenty of precious minerals in the Idarado. It may only be a matter of metal prices rising until the mine opens again.

The Camp Bird Mine was worked off and on until the early 1990s. It usually showed a profit, but the owners eventually gave up on the mine and declared it played out. In 1995 its mill was dismantled and shipped to Mongolia. Geologists declare that there are still rich veins left in the mine. The only local mine working at present is the Grizzly Bear on Bear Creek Trail. A new access tunnel was recently driven to the old workings from the Ouray amphitheater. It was always known that the mine had lots of rich ore in place, but access was a problem that has been solved by the new tunnel. Its owners are blocking out the ore and waiting for a rise in metal prices before they start shipping the ore.

Today, jeeping in the high mountains around Ouray is a favorite pastime. Not only is the scenery fantastic, but relics of by-gone days are scattered throughout the mountains.

With mining basically gone, a good deal of Ouray's economy now revolves around tourism. In the early 1950s the arrival of the little WWII jeep changed local life drastically. The four wheel vehicles made it possible to drive the old wagon roads and, thereby, opened up a part of the back country that up until that time had been seen only by a few brave and hardy souls. The amazing scenery, which includes the ruins of all the old ghost towns and mines, can now be seen by virtually everyone. Ice climbing has also become a popular winter pastime. Water is sprayed down the sides of the Uncompahgre Canyon and climbers from around the world come for the perfect winter conditions provided by Ouray's ice. The climbers also love to soak in the hot springs pool, which is now open all year. As Ouray heads into the twentieth century, it faces a new round of problems. Geologists believe there to be almost as much ore left in the mountains as has already been extracted. When metal prices rise enough, there will be great pressure for the mines to reopen. Yet environmentalists will certainly fight to save what many believe to be the most beautiful spot on the earth. The Ouray tourist industry brings over a hundred thousand visitors in the summer, yet its streets are nearly deserted in the winter; no one yet has solved the problem of bringing in winter tourists without destroying the local atmosphere. Many people wish to move to Ouray, yet locals wish to avoid a building boom. Restrictive zoning practices have, therefore, driven up land prices, making it hard for even the middle class to live in Ouray. Hopefully Ouray will be able to deal with the problems of the future as well as it has dealt with the challenges of the past.

Bibliography

Bauer, W. H., J. L. Ozment and J. H. Willard, **Colorado Postal History: The Post Offices,** J. B. Publishing Co, Crete, Nebraska, 1971.

Benham, J. L., **The Camp Bird and the Revenue,** Bear Creek Publishing Co., Ouray, Colorado, 1880.

Benham, Jack, **Ouray, Colorado,** Bear Creek Publishing Co., Ouray, 1976

Borland, Dr. Lois, "Ouray Remembered", Vol. 37, No. 3, July, 1960, **Colorado Magazine.**

Campbell, Gordon, "Traintime in Ouray", Colorado Railroad Museum, **Colorado Rail Annual — Issue Number Eleven,** Golden, Colorado, 1973.

Croffutt, George A., **Croffutt's Grip -Sack Guide to Colorado,** Omaha, Nebraska, The Overland Publishing Co., 1885.

Crum, Josie, **Ouray County, Colorado,** San Juan History, Inc., Durango, Colorado, 1962.

D. A. R., Sarah Platt Decker Chapter, **Pioneers of the San Juan Country,** Outwest Printing Co., Colorado Springs, Colorado, 1942.

Darley, Rev. George M, **Pioneering in the San Juan,** Fleming H. Revell Co., Chicago, Illinois, 1899.

Day, George Vest, "Momentos of the Dave Day Family", **The 1961 Brand Book,** Vol. 17, The Denver Westerner's Inc., Denver, Colorado, 1962.

Ferrell, Mallory Hope, **Silver San Juan,** Boulder, Colorado, Pruett Publishing Co., 1973.

Fossett, Frank, **Colorado, Its Gold and Silver Mines,** N. Y., N. Y. , C. G. Crawford, 1880.

Gibbons, Rev. J. J., **In the San Juan, Colorado,** Chicago, Illinois, Calmuet Book and Engraving Co., 1898.

Gregory, Marvin and P. David Smith, **Mountain Mysteries,** Ouray, Colorado, Wayfinder Press, 1984.

Gregory, Marvin and P. David Smith, **The Million Dollar Highway,** Ouray, Colorado, Wayfinder Press, 1986.

Hall, C. L., **Resources, Industries and Advantages of Ouray County, Colorado ,** No publisher, No date.

Hall, Frank, **History of the State of Colorado,** Vol. 2, Chicago, Illinois, The Blakely Printing Co., 1890.

Hayden, F. A. , U. S. **Geological and Geographical Survey of Colorado,** Washington, D. C. , 1875, 1876.

Ingersol, Ernest, **The Silver San Juans,** Reprint, Olympic Valley, Calif., Outbooks, 1977.

Ingersol, Ernest, **The Crest of the Continent,** Reprint, Glorieta, N. M., The Rio Grande Press, 1883.

Jocknick, Sidney, **Early Days on the Western Slope,** Glorieta, N. M., The Rio Grande Press, 1913.

Kaplan, Michael, "Colorado's Little Big Man", **Western States Jewish Historical Quarterly 4,** April, 1972.

Kaplan, Michael, Otto Mears, **The Paradoxical Pathfinder,** Silverton, Colorado, San Juan County Book Company, 1982.

Kushner, Ervan, **A Guide to Mineral Collecting at Ouray,** Colorado, Paterson, N. J., Ervan Kushner Books, 1972.

Lavender, David, **One Man's West,** Garden City, New York, Doubleday & Co., 1943.

Marshall, John B. and Temple H. Cornelius, **Golden Treasures of the San Juan,** Denver, Colorado, Sage Books, 1961.

McClean, Evalyn Walsh, **Father Struck It Rich,** Boston, Mass., Little, Brown & Co., 1936.

Monroe, Arthur W., **San Juan Silver,** Montrose, Colorado, Self Published, 1940.

Ouray County Plaindealer, "Ouray Centennial-Historic Souvenir Issue", Ouray, Colorado, 1976.

Rathmell, William, "History of Ouray", Unpublished Manuscript, Ouray, Colorado, undated.

Rice, Frank A., "A History of Ouray and Ouray County", Unpublished Manuscript, Ouray, Colo.,1961.

Rickard, T. A., **Across The San Juan Mountains,** San Francisco, Calif., Mining and Scientific Press, 1907.

Ripley, Henry, **Handclasp of the East and West,** Denver, Williamson-Haffner, 1914.

Rockwell, Wilson, **Sunset Slope,** Denver, Colo., Big Mountain Press, 1956.

Rockwell, Wilson, **Uncompahgre Country,** Denver, Colo., Sage Books, 1965.

Sabin, Edwin L., **Around the Circle,** Reprint, Colorado Springs, Colo., Century One Press, 1913.

Schulze, Suzanne, **A Century of Colorado Census,** Greeley, Colo., University of Northern Colorado, 1976.

Sloan, Robert and Carl A. Scowronski, **The Rainbow Route,** Denver, Colo., Sundance, Ltd., 1975.

Smith, Duane A., "The San Juaner: A Computerized Portrait", **Colorado Magazine** 52, No. 2 (Spring 1975).

Smith, Duane A., **Song of the Hammer and Drill,** Golden, Colorado, Colorado School of Mines Press, 1977.

Smith, P. David, **Mountains of Silver: The Story of Colorado's Red Mountain Mining District,** Boulder, Colo., Pruett Publishing Co., 1994.

Smith, P. David, **Ouray: Chief of the Utes,** Ouray, Colorado, Wayfinder Press, 1986.

Stone, Wilbur F., **History of Colorado,** 4 vols., Chicago, Ill., Clarke Publishing Co., 1918.

Thomas, Chauncey, "Ouray, Opal of America", **Colorado Magazine,** Vol. II, No. 1, January, 1934.

Vandebusche, Duane and Duane A. Smith, **A Land Alone: Colorado's Western Slope,** Boulder, Colo., Pruett Publishing Co., 1981.

Williams, Henry T., **Tourist Guide and Map of the San Juan Mountains of Colorado,** Denver, Colo., Cubar Reprint, 1965.

Williamson, Ruby G., **Otto Mears, Pathfinder of the San Juan,** Gunnison, Colo., B & B Printers, 1981.

Wolle, Muriel Sibell, **Stampede to Timberline,** Chicago, Ill., Swallow Press, 1974.

Wolle, Muriel Sibell, **Timberline Tailings,** Chicago, Ill., Swallow Press, 1977.

Wood, Dorothy and Frances Wood, **I Hauled These Mountains in Here,** Caldwell, Idaho, The Caxton printers, 1977. enry T. HH